GREAT SOURCE

Test Achiever

Mastering Standardized Tests

Grade 8

Test preparation for reading,
language arts, and mathematics

GReaT SOuRCe
EDUCATION GROUP
A Houghton Mifflin Company

Great Source® is a registered trademark of Houghton Mifflin Company.

Design and production by Publicom, Inc., Acton, Massachusetts

Printed in the United States of America

International Standard Book Number: 0-669-46464-3

    6 7 8 9 10 - HS - 03 02

URL address: http://www.greatsource.com/

READING: Vocabulary

Directions: Find the word that means the same, or almost the same, as the underlined word.

1. new <u>attire</u>

   Ⓐ plan   Ⓒ belief

   Ⓑ clothing   Ⓓ address

2. a <u>festive</u> gathering

   Ⓐ large   Ⓒ merry

   Ⓑ formal   Ⓓ somber

3. to <u>barter</u>

   Ⓐ cut   Ⓒ chat

   Ⓑ tease   Ⓓ trade

4. a great <u>humiliation</u>

   Ⓐ embarrassment

   Ⓑ honor

   Ⓒ awakening

   Ⓓ duty

5. <u>punctured</u> the tire

   Ⓐ repaired   Ⓒ adjusted

   Ⓑ pierced   Ⓓ tested

6. a <u>dominant</u> team

   Ⓐ competitive   Ⓒ controlling

   Ⓑ young   Ⓓ weak

Directions: Find the word that means the OPPOSITE of the underlined word.

7. very <u>naive</u>

   Ⓐ sophisticated   Ⓒ casual

   Ⓑ innocent   Ⓓ rude

8. <u>despised</u> by many

   Ⓐ known   Ⓒ disliked

   Ⓑ loved   Ⓓ remembered

9. a feeling of <u>optimism</u>

   Ⓐ happiness   Ⓒ confusion

   Ⓑ pride   Ⓓ hopelessness

Directions: Read the two sentences. Find the word that best fits the meaning of **both** sentences.

10. The poem continues on the next _____.

   We will _____ you if we need you.

   Ⓐ verse   Ⓒ page

   Ⓑ call   Ⓓ find

11. The table is one _____ wide.

   The _____ indicates that the fuel tank is nearly empty.

   Ⓐ yard   Ⓒ length

   Ⓑ gauge   Ⓓ meter

12. He lives in a _____ area.

Where is the _____ control for the TV?

- (A) remote
- (C) channel
- (B) distant
- (D) volume

13. Denise has always been a _____ sleeper.

Can you shed any _____ on this mystery?

- (A) restless
- (C) sound
- (B) clue
- (D) light

Directions: Read the sentence and the question. Find the word that best answers the question.

14. The librarian _____ at the noisy students.

Which word suggests that the librarian was annoyed?

- (A) gazed
- (B) looked
- (C) glared
- (D) peeked

15. James and Leanne _____ snowballs at our fort.

Which word suggests the use of force?

- (A) hurled
- (B) tossed
- (C) threw
- (D) lobbed

Directions: Read the sentences. Choose the word that best completes the meaning of each sentence.

Mrs. Ross was driving down the highway. Suddenly the traffic __(16)__ to a crawl. Since Mrs. Ross was __(17)__ a freight truck, she could not see what was causing the problem ahead. When the traffic came to a complete __(18)__, Mrs. Ross sighed impatiently. She had only ten minutes to get to her dentist's __(19)__. She did not want to be __(20)__ for her appointment.

16.
- (A) turned
- (C) slowed
- (B) signaled
- (D) exited

17.
- (A) behind
- (C) inside
- (B) near
- (D) around

18.
- (A) intersection
- (C) curve
- (B) speed
- (D) halt

19.
- (A) realm
- (C) vehicle
- (B) office
- (D) examination

20.
- (A) tardy
- (C) tired
- (B) nervous
- (D) surprised

READING: Comprehension

Directions: Read each passage. Choose the best answer to each question.

Fish or Mammal?

Is a dolphin a fish or a mammal? With their flippers, fins, and furless bodies, dolphins are easily mistaken for fish. But dolphins are born live, rather than in eggs, and are nursed by their mothers. They are also warm-blooded. These traits mean that dolphins belong to the mammal family.

Fish and dolphins also differ in the way they breathe. Fish absorb oxygen directly from the water through their gills, but dolphins breathe with lungs. They must hold their breath underwater and come to the surface for air.

But dolphins do not need to "take a breather" as often as you might think. Unlike other mammal swimmers, such as beavers and seals, dolphins have the ability to stretch their oxygen supply. They can direct oxygen only to the most important organs—the heart and the brain. They can also slow down their heart rate so they burn up less oxygen. By using oxygen so efficiently, dolphins can stay underwater for more than ten minutes at a time.

---

21. This passage is mostly about –

- Ⓐ common mammals
- Ⓑ characteristics of dolphins
- Ⓒ habits of fish
- Ⓓ ocean life

22. Which statement is an opinion?

- Ⓐ Dolphins are easily mistaken for fish.
- Ⓑ Dolphins are mammals.
- Ⓒ Dolphins must hold their breath underwater.
- Ⓓ Dolphins can stretch their oxygen supply.

23. Dolphins are most like fish in that they –

- Ⓐ breathe with their lungs
- Ⓑ bear live babies
- Ⓒ have fins and furless bodies
- Ⓓ slow their heart rate

24. Which conclusion can be drawn from this passage?

- Ⓐ Mammals are more common than fish.
- Ⓑ Beavers and seals are warm-blooded.
- Ⓒ Some fish must surface for air.
- Ⓓ A dolphin has a small brain.

Put to the Test

Heather had been lab partners with Penny McKay since the first day of Mr. Carlson's biology class. In the beginning, Heather was flattered that Penny asked to be her partner. With her bubbly personality and glamorous good looks, Penny was easily the most popular girl in the eighth grade. Perhaps being partners will give us a chance to become friends, Heather thought. And she began to daydream about how she would soon be part of Penny's crowd.

By the middle of October, things had changed. The idea that Heather would become Penny's friend was obviously just pie in the sky. The party invitations had never come, and Penny completely ignored Heather outside the classroom. Penny was friendly enough during biology class, but only for a self-serving reason: she was copying Heather's work.

Heather was aware of Penny's wandering eyes almost from the start, but she did not say anything. In fact, she had not really minded having such a popular girl think her work was worth copying. But now Heather was paying an unexpected price. When Mr. Carlson noticed that the girls' lab reports were just too similar, he drew his own conclusion about who was copying from whom. Each time he corrected lab reports, he marked Penny's one grade higher than Heather's.

When Heather realized what was happening, she felt furious—and helpless. She ruled out trying to talk to Mr. Carlson; since he had already decided she was the cheater, it would be hard to change his mind. And Heather knew she could not confront Penny. She just did not have the gumption to stand up to the leader of the popular crowd. Still, Heather was not about to let Penny rob her of the B or B+ she deserved to get from Mr. Carlson. With an important test coming up the next week, Heather decided to show Mr. Carlson that she, not Penny, was the one doing the honest work.

On the day of the test, Penny took her seat beside Heather and gave her a nervous smile. Then Mr. Carlson passed out the tests. Even as Heather wrote her name at the top, she could sense Penny's cautious sidelong glances, which continued as Heather worked her way through the test. Not surprisingly, the two girls finished at the same time. But while Penny immediately stood up to turn in her test, Heather held onto hers. When Heather saw Mr. Carlson pick up Penny's test and start to correct it, she began methodically to erase the answers she had written on her test. Now she was ready to write the correct answers.

25. What do you think will happen next?

  (A) Penny will fail the test.

  (B) Penny will become friendly with Heather.

  (C) Mr. Carlson will tell Heather to stop copying from Penny.

  (D) Heather will have trouble answering the test questions.

26. What does this story reveal about Heather?

  (A) She cared more about being popular than being a good student.

  (B) She had trouble standing up for herself.

  (C) She was unattractive.

  (D) She had a reputation as a hardworking student.

27. The idea that Heather would become Penny's friend was "pie in the sky" means that it was –

  (A) a great temptation

  (B) a worthwhile goal

  (C) a dream coming true

  (D) an unrealistic hope

28. This story is narrated by –

  (A) Penny

  (B) Mr. Carlson

  (C) Heather

  (D) an outside observer

29. What bothered Heather most about what Penny was doing?

  (A) She was never invited to Penny's parties.

  (B) Penny ignored her outside of class.

  (C) Mr. Carlson assumed that she was copying from Penny.

  (D) Penny was a popular girl.

30. When did Heather decide to do something about Penny's cheating?

  (A) as soon as she noticed it

  (B) just before an important test

  (C) after she got a B+ grade

  (D) when Penny started making fun of her

31. Heather solved her problem by –

  (A) reporting Penny's cheating to Mr. Carlson

  (B) asking to have a new lab partner

  (C) writing wrong answers for Penny to copy

  (D) keeping Penny from seeing her test

32. The theme of this story is mainly concerned with –

  (A) being honest

  (B) how to become popular

  (C) being envious

  (D) how to avoid cheaters

The Vegetarian Way

Until the age of 13, Frank was perfectly content to eat meals made with meat. He had even learned to prepare his favorite chicken burritos by himself. But then Frank read an article that aroused his sympathy for animals that are raised only for food. After that, he resolved to become a vegetarian.

Frank's parents tried to help him although they did not know much about vegetarianism. They stocked the refrigerator with fresh fruits and vegetables, but Frank did not eat much of them. Instead, he ate a lot of peanut butter-and-jelly sandwiches, brownies, and pastries. Before long he was feeling run-down and cranky most of the time.

Many young people who become vegetarians have experiences like Frank's—not because vegetarianism is unhealthful, but because they do not know how to be healthy vegetarians. Meat supplies the body with significant amounts of protein, iron, vitamin B-12, and other essential nutrients. So when vegetarians exclude meat from their diets, they must be careful to substitute other foods rich in these nutrients. Pastas, grains, and legumes, such as peas and beans, are staples in a balanced vegetarian diet.

Once Frank learned this lesson, he enjoyed his decision to become a vegetarian. And he learned to prepare a new favorite—bean burritos.

33. The author's main purpose in this passage is to —

(A) tell an entertaining story

(B) give information

(C) compare meat and vegetables

(D) criticize vegetarians

34. Frank "resolved to become a vegetarian." Resolved means —

(A) decided

(B) attempted

(C) pretended

(D) hoped

35. Frank felt run-down because he —

(A) ate too many fruits and vegetables

(B) gained too much weight

(C) still ate meat once in a while

(D) was not getting important nutrients

36. Which is the best summary of this passage?

(A) Frank read an article that convinced him to become a vegetarian.

(B) Frank became a vegetarian, but he had trouble until he included foods containing certain nutrients.

(C) Frank used to eat meat and fish, but now he eats pastas and legumes.

(D) Frank would not have had so much trouble becoming a vegetarian if his parents had known more about it.

LANGUAGE ARTS: Mechanics and Usage

Directions: Read each sentence. Look at the underlined part for a mistake in capitalization, punctuation, or word usage. If you find a mistake, choose the best way to write the underlined part of the sentence. If there is no mistake, fill in the bubble beside answer D, "Correct as is."

1. The tomato plants <u>growed</u> quickly.

   Ⓐ grew   Ⓒ grown

   Ⓑ growing   Ⓓ Correct as is

2. Jerry <u>is feeling</u> sick for two days before he went to the doctor.

   Ⓐ has been feeling

   Ⓑ feels

   Ⓒ had felt

   Ⓓ Correct as is

3. Either Zena or Julie will take <u>her</u> turn next.

   Ⓐ their   Ⓒ them

   Ⓑ hers   Ⓓ Correct as is

4. The gymnast did the <u>difficultest</u> routine I've ever seen.

   Ⓐ more difficult   Ⓒ most difficult

   Ⓑ difficulter   Ⓓ Correct as is

5. Jodi <u>couldn't hardly</u> talk.

   Ⓐ could hardly not

   Ⓑ could hardly

   Ⓒ hardly couldn't

   Ⓓ Correct as is

6. <u>Quartz, one</u> of the hardest minerals, is used to make sandpaper.

   Ⓐ Quartz one   Ⓒ Quartz; one

   Ⓑ Quartz: one   Ⓓ Correct as is

7. My aunt lives in <u>Green hills</u> Tennessee.

   Ⓐ Green hills,   Ⓒ Green Hills,

   Ⓑ Green Hills   Ⓓ Correct as is

8. We are both in <u>Ms Jones</u> class.

   Ⓐ Ms. Jones's   Ⓒ Ms. Jones

   Ⓑ Ms Jones'   Ⓓ Correct as is

9. Jim works at the <u>Quality Paper company</u>.

   Ⓐ quality paper company

   Ⓑ Quality paper company

   Ⓒ Quality Paper Company

   Ⓓ Correct as is

10. Mr. Ames said, <u>please call me.</u>

    Ⓐ "please call me."

    Ⓑ "Please call me."

    Ⓒ Please call me.

    Ⓓ Correct as is

11. My mother loves <u>*the wizard of Oz*</u>.

    Ⓐ *The Wizard Of Oz*

    Ⓑ *The Wizard of Oz*

    Ⓒ *the wizard of oz*

    Ⓓ Correct as is

LANGUAGE ARTS: Mechanics and Usage (continued)

Directions: Read the sentences. Find the underlined word that has a mistake in spelling. If there are no mistakes in spelling, fill in the bubble beside answer D, "No mistake."

12. Ⓐ Henry checked the <u>calander</u>.
    Ⓑ His <u>research</u> report was due.
    Ⓒ He was far behind <u>schedule</u>.
    Ⓓ No mistake

13. Ⓐ We got to the <u>gymnasium</u> at noon.
    Ⓑ The <u>custodian</u> let us in.
    Ⓒ The rest of our <u>teamates</u> arrived.
    Ⓓ No mistake

14. Ⓐ You cannot see the earth's <u>equator</u>.
    Ⓑ It is an <u>imaginery</u> line.
    Ⓒ It <u>separates</u> two hemispheres.
    Ⓓ No mistake

15. Ⓐ She gave her <u>acceptance</u> speech.
    Ⓑ She thanked the <u>campaign</u> workers.
    Ⓒ Most of them were <u>volunteers</u>.
    Ⓓ No mistake

16. Ⓐ Mr. Katz opened a new <u>business</u>.
    Ⓑ He repairs <u>electronic</u> equipment.
    Ⓒ He is <u>advertizing</u> in the newspaper.
    Ⓓ No mistake

17. Ⓐ That is not a <u>genuwin</u> skeleton.
    Ⓑ It is a plaster <u>reproduction</u>.
    Ⓒ The museum sells a smaller <u>version</u>.
    Ⓓ No mistake

Directions: Find the answer that is a complete sentence written correctly.

18. Ⓐ This messy page of math homework.
    Ⓑ Smears left by a dirty eraser.
    Ⓒ Even a tear from erasing too much.
    Ⓓ At least the answers are correct.

19. Ⓐ The last rain slicker in the store.
    Ⓑ It's an ugly green no wonder no one has bought it.
    Ⓒ Remembering the last big rainstorm.
    Ⓓ I don't want to get drenched again.

20. Ⓐ The flu has been going around lately.
    Ⓑ Dad caught it first he felt awful for two days.
    Ⓒ My brother next and then me.
    Ⓓ Mom was fine she never got sick.

21. Ⓐ Two new eighth-graders this year.
    Ⓑ Probably nervous on their first day.
    Ⓒ They introduced themselves to the class.
    Ⓓ Trying to remember their names.

22. Ⓐ That burning smell coming from the kitchen.
    Ⓑ The smoke detector will go off in a second.
    Ⓒ The toast burned it did not pop up.
    Ⓓ Settling for some corn flakes instead.

LANGUAGE ARTS: Composition

Directions: Read each paragraph. Then answer the questions that follow.

Paragraph 1

It is also an ability that varies from person to person. At one end of the scale are people who have excellent memories for details. Sometimes a head injury can cause a loss of memory. At the other end are those who cannot recall the names of people they see every day. They may also forget the names of places they see every day. Most of us fall somewhere between these two extremes. But even for a poor memory, there are ways to improve your poor memory.

---

23. What is the best topic sentence for this paragraph?

Ⓐ Scientists have answered many questions about how memory works.

Ⓑ Memory is the ability to keep a mental record of your experiences.

Ⓒ Memory can be triggered by sound.

Ⓓ Repeated actions or routines are generally easy to remember.

24. What is the best way to combine the fourth and fifth sentences?

Ⓐ At the other end are those who cannot recall the names of people or places they see every day.

Ⓑ Those at the other end cannot recall the names of people and places.

Ⓒ At the other end are those who see people and places every day.

Ⓓ Those who cannot recall the places they see and the people every day are at the other end.

25. Which sentence does **not** belong in this paragraph?

Ⓐ It is also an ability that varies from person to person.

Ⓑ At one end of the scale are people who have excellent memories for details.

Ⓒ Sometimes a head injury can cause a loss of memory.

Ⓓ Most of us fall somewhere between these two extremes.

26. Which is the best way to revise the last sentence?

Ⓐ But for a poor memory, there are ways.

Ⓑ There are some poor ways to improve your memory.

Ⓒ Some ways to improve your memory will give you a poor memory.

Ⓓ But even a poor memory can be improved.

Paragraph 2

But parents should realize that even the most mature teen needs basic information and guidelines to do a good job caring for young children. Most important, leave a telephone number. It should be the number where you can be reached. Lay out clothes or pajamas that will be needed, and tell the sitter what foods children may or may not eat. Specify bedtimes and describe any going-to-bed routines children may have. Finally, make it clear that the baby-sitter may not have company.

---

27. What is the best topic sentence for this paragraph?

(A) Grandparents or teens are popular choices for baby-sitters.

(B) You can actually take a course to learn how to be a baby-sitter.

(C) A responsible teenager can be a terrific baby-sitter for young children.

(D) Baby-sitting for young children can be fun and rewarding.

28. What is the best way to combine the second and third sentences?

(A) Most important, leave the telephone number where you can be reached.

(B) Leave the most important telephone number where you can be reached.

(C) Most important, where you can be reached, leave your telephone number.

(D) Where you can be reached is an important telephone number to leave.

29. Which sentence would fit best at the end of this paragraph?

(A) Many parents did baby-sitting as teenagers.

(B) Children might expect a story or song at bedtime.

(C) You might also leave the number of a neighbor to call in case of an emergency.

(D) Having friends around could distract your sitter's attention from the children.

30. This paragraph was probably written for what audience?

(A) young children

(B) young children's parents

(C) teenagers

(D) schoolteachers

LANGUAGE ARTS: Study Skills

Directions: Choose the best answer to each question about finding information.

31. If you wanted to learn about the climate, economy, and history of Nigeria, you should look in –

Ⓐ an atlas   Ⓒ an encyclopedia
Ⓑ a thesaurus   Ⓓ a dictionary

32. Which of these is a main heading that includes the other topics?

Ⓐ Music   Ⓒ Jazz
Ⓑ Composer   Ⓓ Orchestra

33. To find every page in a book where a specific topic is mentioned, you should look in the –

Ⓐ bibliography   Ⓒ title page
Ⓑ index   Ⓓ table of contents

34. To find a book about Sir Winston Churchill, a prime minister of Great Britain, you should look in an online library catalog under –

Ⓐ Sir   Ⓒ Minister
Ⓑ Churchill   Ⓓ Britain

35. The word *consider* might be found on a dictionary page with which guide words?

Ⓐ convex/cooper
Ⓑ connect/conquest
Ⓒ conserve/consist
Ⓓ conspire/contact

Use the schedule to answer questions 36–38.

Schedule of Classes at The Arts Center

Class	Teacher	Time	Room
Ceramics	Ms. Lopez	8:30 A.M.	301
Drawing	Mr. Franklin	10:15 A.M.	304
Sculpture	Ms. Lopez	11:30 A.M.	301
Painting	Mrs. Taft	1:15 P.M.	302
Photography	Mr. Kroll	2:00 P.M.	303

36. At what time is a drawing class held at The Arts Center?

Ⓐ 8:30 A.M.   Ⓒ 1:15 P.M.
Ⓑ 10:15 A.M.   Ⓓ 2:00 P.M.

37. What two classes are taught by Ms. Lopez?

Ⓐ Ceramics and Drawing
Ⓑ Sculpture and Painting
Ⓒ Photography and Painting
Ⓓ Ceramics and Sculpture

38. In what room is the Photography class held?

Ⓐ Room 301   Ⓒ Room 303
Ⓑ Room 302   Ⓓ Room 304

Stop

MATHEMATICS: Concepts and Applications

Directions: Choose the best answer to each question.

1. What is 89,321 rounded to the nearest thousand?

   Ⓐ 90,000   Ⓒ 89,300

   Ⓑ 89,500   Ⓓ 89,000

2. What number is expressed by 2,000,000 + 300,000 + 5000 + 40 + 7?

   Ⓐ 2,354,700   Ⓒ 235,047

   Ⓑ 2,305,047   Ⓓ 23,547

3. $(4 \times 10^3) + (1 \times 10^2) + (2 \times 10^1) + (8 \times 10^0) =$

   Ⓐ 4,001,028   Ⓒ 4128

   Ⓑ 40,128   Ⓓ 412.8

4. What number completes this pattern?

   2, 5, 11, __?__ , 47, . . .

   Ⓐ 18   Ⓒ 23

   Ⓑ 22   Ⓓ 28

5. Which expresses the number 150 in prime factors?

   Ⓐ $5 \times 5 \times 6$

   Ⓑ $3 \times 5 \times 10$

   Ⓒ $2 \times 3 \times 5 \times 5$

   Ⓓ 10×15

6. What is the least common multiple of 6, 7, and 11?

   Ⓐ 42   Ⓒ 462

   Ⓑ 77   Ⓓ 1386

7. What is the square root of 5184?

   Ⓐ 9   Ⓒ 56

   Ⓑ 17   Ⓓ 72

8. Which fraction is least?

   Ⓐ $\frac{2}{7}$

   Ⓑ $\frac{3}{5}$

   Ⓒ $\frac{4}{12}$

   Ⓓ $\frac{6}{15}$

9. Which fraction is another name for $13\frac{7}{8}$?

   Ⓐ $\frac{111}{8}$

   Ⓑ $\frac{99}{7}$

   Ⓒ $\frac{28}{8}$

   Ⓓ $\frac{20}{7}$

10. Which percent has the same value as $\frac{4}{25}$?

    Ⓐ 10%

    Ⓑ 16%

    Ⓒ 21%

    Ⓓ 29%

MATHEMATICS: Concepts and Applications (continued)

11. Which number has the greatest value?

Ⓐ 0.0783 Ⓒ 0.642

Ⓑ 0.129 Ⓓ 0.4931

12. The **5** in 36.0715 represents —

Ⓐ 5 tenths

Ⓑ 5 hundredths

Ⓒ 5 thousandths

Ⓓ 5 ten thousandths

13. What is 76.3081 rounded to the nearest hundredth?

Ⓐ 76.0 Ⓒ 76.31

Ⓑ 76.3 Ⓓ 76.308

14. The arrow points to what number on the number line?

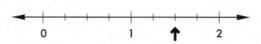

Ⓐ $1\frac{1}{4}$

Ⓑ $1\frac{1}{2}$

Ⓒ $1\frac{3}{4}$

Ⓓ 6

15. If $4x + 7 = 27$, then $x =$

Ⓐ 8

Ⓑ 6

Ⓒ 5

Ⓓ 3

16. If $b \times c = 56$, then which of these statements is true?

Ⓐ $56 \div c = b$

Ⓑ $b \times 56 = c$

Ⓒ $56 - b = c$

Ⓓ $b \div c = 56$

17. Which number goes in the box to make this sentence true?

$24(13 + 8) = (24 \times \square) + (24 \times 8)$

Ⓐ 5 Ⓒ 11

Ⓑ 8 Ⓓ 13

18. Which point on the grid represents $(1, {}^-2)$?

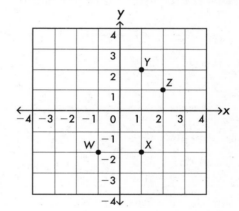

Ⓐ W Ⓒ Y

Ⓑ X Ⓓ Z

19. Which two figures are similar?

Ⓐ

Ⓑ

Ⓒ

Ⓓ

20. In this figure, which line segment is parallel to $\overline{EC}$?

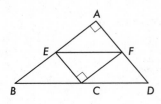

(A) $\overline{AD}$

(C) $\overline{CF}$

(B) $\overline{BD}$

(D) $\overline{EF}$

21. Which type of angle is equal to 90°?

(A) acute

(C) obtuse

(B) right

(D) straight

22. What is the perimeter of this figure?

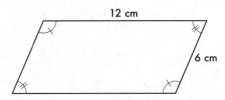

(A) 18 cm

(C) 36 cm

(B) 24 cm

(D) 54 cm

23. What is the area of this triangle?

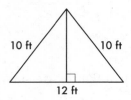

(A) 30 ft²

(C) 48 ft²

(B) 32 ft²

(D) 60 ft²

24. What is the volume of this figure?

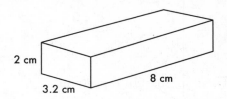

(A) 102.4 cm³

(C) 25.6 cm³

(B) 51.2 cm³

(D) 13.2 cm³

25. If $\angle DBE = 50°$, what is the size of $\angle ABD$?

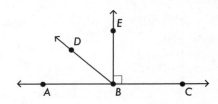

(A) 20°

(C) 40°

(B) 30°

(D) 50°

26. How many pints are in $2\frac{1}{2}$ gallons of milk?

(A) 10 pints

(C) 16 pints

(B) 12 pints

(D) 20 pints

27. A camel went for 228 hours without water. How long is this period in weeks and days?

(A) 1 week $2\frac{1}{2}$ days

(B) 1 week 5 days

(C) 9 weeks 5 days

(D) 9 weeks $2\frac{1}{2}$ days

MATHEMATICS: Concepts and Applications (continued)

Directions: Solve each problem. If the correct answer is Not Given, mark answer D, "NG."

28. Liza played a game at the video arcade. Her scores were 373, 431, 319, 404, and 398. What was Liza's median score?

Ⓐ 385   Ⓒ 401

Ⓑ 398   Ⓓ NG

29. A computer copies 4.5 megabytes of data in 10 seconds. At this rate, how long will it take to copy 36 megabytes of data?

Ⓐ 360 sec   Ⓒ 80 sec

Ⓑ 180 sec   Ⓓ NG

30. Mr. Crosby commutes 56 miles each day he works. If his car gets 18 to 22 miles per gallon of gasoline, about how many gallons will he use in 5 days?

Ⓐ 15   Ⓒ 8

Ⓑ 10   Ⓓ 7

31. In a drawing for a bicycle, Hank has 12 tickets and Wanda has 20. If one ticket is drawn from 416 entries, what is the probability that either Hank or Wanda will win?

Ⓐ $\frac{1}{52}$ Ⓒ $\frac{1}{8}$

Ⓑ $\frac{1}{32}$ Ⓓ NG

32. A wool sweater costs \$39.90, but a customer who buys two sweaters gets the second one at a 40% discount. What is the cost of two sweaters?

Ⓐ \$71.82   Ⓒ \$55.86

Ⓑ \$63.84   Ⓓ NG

Use the line graph below to answer 33–34.

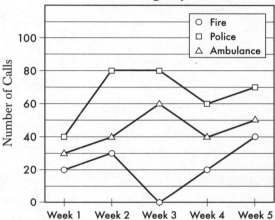

33. In which week were the fewest calls made for a police emergency?

Ⓐ Week 1   Ⓒ Week 3

Ⓑ Week 2   Ⓓ Week 4

34. What was the total number of emergency calls made during Week 2?

Ⓐ 140   Ⓒ 160

Ⓑ 150   Ⓓ NG

Stop

Pretest

MATHEMATICS: Computation

Directions: Find the answer to each problem. If the correct answer is Not Given, mark answer D, "NG."

35.
$$31,425$$
$$- 29,497$$

   Ⓐ 2038
   Ⓑ 1928
   Ⓒ 1078
   Ⓓ NG

36. $432.007 + 12.0913 =$
   Ⓐ 444.0983
   Ⓑ 552.92
   Ⓒ 1641.137
   Ⓓ NG

37. $27\overline{)54,026}$
   Ⓐ 200 R6
   Ⓑ 2001
   Ⓒ 2000 R26
   Ⓓ NG

38. $41.02 \times 50 =$
   Ⓐ 20,510
   Ⓑ 2052
   Ⓒ 2050.1
   Ⓓ NG

39. $8.50\overline{)\$386.75}$
   Ⓐ $4450.00
   Ⓑ $455.00
   Ⓒ $45.50
   Ⓓ NG

40. $12.05 \times {}^-8 =$
   Ⓐ $^-964$
   Ⓑ $^-96.4$
   Ⓒ 96.4
   Ⓓ NG

41. $\frac{14}{3} + 7\frac{2}{5} =$
   Ⓐ $7\frac{6}{15}$
   Ⓑ $11\frac{1}{2}$
   Ⓒ $12\frac{1}{15}$
   Ⓓ NG

42. $(^-21 + 6) - 4 =$
   Ⓐ $^-31$
   Ⓑ $^-23$
   Ⓒ $^-19$
   Ⓓ NG

43. $13\frac{3}{4} \times \frac{5}{6} =$
   Ⓐ $11\frac{1}{2}$
   Ⓑ $12\frac{1}{12}$
   Ⓒ $12\frac{13}{24}$
   Ⓓ NG

44. $\frac{5}{9} \div \frac{1}{3} =$
   Ⓐ $\frac{5}{27}$
   Ⓑ $1\frac{2}{3}$
   Ⓒ $1\frac{3}{5}$
   Ⓓ NG

45. $27 = \square\% \text{ of } 540$
   Ⓐ 5
   Ⓑ 15
   Ⓒ 20
   Ⓓ NG

46. $35\% \text{ of } 250 =$
   Ⓐ 875
   Ⓑ 87.5
   Ⓒ 8.75
   Ⓓ NG

Stop

PRACTICE 1 • Synonyms and Antonyms

SAMPLES

Directions: Choose the word that means the same, or almost the same, as the underlined word.

A. <u>legible</u> handwriting

    Ⓐ cursive   Ⓒ readable

    Ⓑ messy   Ⓓ capital

Directions: Choose the word that means the OPPOSITE of the underlined word.

B. a <u>repulsive</u> person

    Ⓐ horrible   Ⓒ attractive

    Ⓑ strange   Ⓓ different

Tips and Reminders

- When looking for a synonym, watch out for answer choices that are related to the underlined word (such as *cursive*) but have different meanings.

- When looking for an antonym, watch out for words that have the same meaning (such as *repulsive* and *horrible*).

PRACTICE

Directions: Choose the word that means the same, or almost the same, as the underlined word.

1. to <u>ensure</u>

    Ⓐ admire

    Ⓑ examine

    Ⓒ recommend

    Ⓓ guarantee

2. of average <u>stature</u>

    Ⓐ height

    Ⓑ age

    Ⓒ intelligence

    Ⓓ strength

3. a <u>persuasive</u> argument

    Ⓐ sympathetic

    Ⓑ convincing

    Ⓒ meaningless

    Ⓓ friendly

4. this <u>pamphlet</u>

    Ⓐ child

    Ⓑ publication

    Ⓒ feature

    Ⓓ cartoon

5. a <u>graphic</u> description

- (A) short
- (B) quick
- (C) vivid
- (D) complex

6. foreign <u>currency</u>

- (A) language
- (B) travel
- (C) country
- (D) money

7. foul <u>stench</u>

- (A) odor
- (B) mood
- (C) breath
- (D) habit

8. <u>variable</u> weather

- (A) stormy
- (B) changing
- (C) predictable
- (D) current

9. to <u>dilate</u>

- (A) expand
- (B) blink
- (C) contract
- (D) behold

10. the <u>penalty</u>

- (A) warning
- (B) regulation
- (C) punishment
- (D) advice

11. to <u>allege</u>

- (A) declare
- (B) deny
- (C) prove
- (D) mock

12. <u>tangible</u> proof

- (A) legal
- (B) false
- (C) honest
- (D) definite

13. will <u>narrate</u>

- (A) invent
- (B) tell
- (C) breathe
- (D) confuse

14. general <u>disorder</u>

- (A) organization
- (B) knowledge
- (C) confusion
- (D) curiosity

15. to <u>merge</u>

- (A) divide
- (B) grasp
- (C) insert
- (D) combine

16. <u>competent</u> lawyer

- (A) shrewd
- (B) capable
- (C) sympathetic
- (D) reasonable

PRACTICE 1 • Synonyms and Antonyms (continued)

Directions: Choose the word that means the OPPOSITE of the underlined word.

17. will <u>extinguish</u>
- Ⓐ pursue
- Ⓑ ignite
- Ⓒ destroy
- Ⓓ confine

18. <u>multiple</u> wounds
- Ⓐ harsh
- Ⓑ fragile
- Ⓒ single
- Ⓓ numerous

19. <u>haggard</u> appearance
- Ⓐ worn
- Ⓑ worried
- Ⓒ exhausted
- Ⓓ hearty

20. vitamin <u>deficiency</u>
- Ⓐ effect
- Ⓑ lack
- Ⓒ surplus
- Ⓓ assistance

21. will <u>transmit</u>
- Ⓐ receive
- Ⓑ discard
- Ⓒ send
- Ⓓ faint

22. his <u>innocence</u>
- Ⓐ goodness
- Ⓑ guilt
- Ⓒ forgiveness
- Ⓓ prejudice

23. to <u>recollect</u>
- Ⓐ surrender
- Ⓑ forget
- Ⓒ recognize
- Ⓓ misplace

24. was <u>passive</u>
- Ⓐ stupid
- Ⓑ offensive
- Ⓒ quiet
- Ⓓ active

25. a <u>trivial</u> matter
- Ⓐ petty
- Ⓑ lengthy
- Ⓒ secret
- Ⓓ important

26. to <u>incite</u>
- Ⓐ suppress
- Ⓑ influence
- Ⓒ foretell
- Ⓓ encourage

27. with <u>malice</u>
- Ⓐ spite
- Ⓑ refuge
- Ⓒ kindness
- Ⓓ intelligence

28. always <u>unkempt</u>
- Ⓐ neat
- Ⓑ wrinkled
- Ⓒ sloppy
- Ⓓ expensive

PRACTICE 2 • Using Verbs

Directions: Read each sentence and look at the underlined part. There may be a mistake in word usage. If you find a mistake, choose the best way to write the underlined part of the sentence. If there is no mistake, fill in the bubble beside answer D, "Correct as is."

SAMPLES

A. Derek <u>finished</u> mowing the lawn tomorrow.

    Ⓐ finish
    Ⓑ finishing
    Ⓒ will finish
    Ⓓ Correct as is

B. Kate and Nathan <u>found</u> a snake under the porch.

    Ⓐ finds
    Ⓑ finded
    Ⓒ is finding
    Ⓓ Correct as is

Tips and Reminders

- Try each answer choice in the sentence to see which one sounds right.
- Be careful with irregular forms of words, such as *found*.
- Watch out for incorrect forms of words, such as *finded*.

PRACTICE

1. Josie and Lydia <u>has been</u> friends for many years.

    Ⓐ is
    Ⓑ was
    Ⓒ have been
    Ⓓ Correct as is

2. This box of pencils <u>are</u> mine.

    Ⓐ is   Ⓒ be
    Ⓑ were   Ⓓ Correct as is

3. Clayton <u>bought</u> himself a new calculator.

    Ⓐ buy   Ⓒ buying
    Ⓑ buyed   Ⓓ Correct as is

4. Trina and I <u>enjoys</u> funny movies.

    Ⓐ enjoy
    Ⓑ is enjoying
    Ⓒ has enjoyed
    Ⓓ Correct as is

5. I <u>must have throwed</u> away my homework by mistake.

   (A) must have throw

   (B) must have thrown

   (C) must have threw

   (D) Correct as is

6. The boys <u>confess</u> to the crime when the police questioned them.

   (A) confessing

   (B) was confessing

   (C) confessed

   (D) Correct as is

7. Ginny <u>writing</u> in her journal every morning.

   (A) write

   (B) writes

   (C) are writing

   (D) Correct as is

8. The warranty on Tim's computer <u>has expired</u> by next week.

   (A) expired

   (B) must have expired

   (C) will have expired

   (D) Correct as is

9. Many patients at the clinic <u>is</u> sick with the flu.

   (A) are

   (B) was

   (C) being

   (D) Correct as is

10. Our pond <u>freezed</u> last week when temperatures dropped below zero.

   (A) freezes

   (B) froze

   (C) frozen

   (D) Correct as is

11. Ted <u>tried to ignore</u> the stray dog, but it followed him home anyway.

   (A) tries to ignore

   (B) trying to ignore

   (C) will try to ignore

   (D) Correct as is

12. Mrs. Kramer <u>haven't told</u> anyone it's her birthday.

   (A) hasn't told

   (B) haven't telled

   (C) hasn't tell

   (D) Correct as is

13. This geranium <u>has outgrew</u> its pot.

   (A) outgrowed

   (B) have outgrown

   (C) has outgrown

   (D) Correct as is

14. The hungry child <u>stealed</u> a loaf of bread yesterday.

   (A) steals

   (B) stole

   (C) will be stealing

   (D) Correct as is

PRACTICE 3 • Whole Number Concepts

Directions: Choose the best answer to each question.

SAMPLES

A. $100,000 + 40,000 + 500 + 8 =$

- Ⓐ 104,508
- Ⓑ 145,800
- Ⓒ 140,580
- Ⓓ 140,508

B. Which is the least common multiple of 3 and 13?

- Ⓐ 3
- Ⓑ 13
- Ⓒ 26
- Ⓓ 39

Tips and Reminders

- Be sure to look at all the answer choices before you choose an answer. Try each answer choice to find the one that is correct.

- After choosing an answer, read the question again to make sure you have answered it correctly.

PRACTICE

1. $2,000,000 + 30,000 + 6000 + 70 =$

- Ⓐ 2,367,000
- Ⓑ 2,306,070
- Ⓒ 2,036,070
- Ⓓ 236,070

2. What number is expressed by $(7 \times 10^4) + (3 \times 10^2) + (5 \times 10) + (4 \times 1)$?

- Ⓐ 73,540
- Ⓒ 7354
- Ⓑ 70,354
- Ⓓ 735.4

3. $5^3 =$

- Ⓐ 125
- Ⓑ 75
- Ⓒ 25
- Ⓓ 15

4. Which is a prime number?

- Ⓐ 9
- Ⓑ 19
- Ⓒ 39
- Ⓓ 91

5. What is the square root of 225?

(A) 12   (C) 45

(B) 15   (D) 450

6. Which is another way to write 6^3?

(A) 6×3

(B) $6 \times (6 + 6)$

(C) $6^2 + 6^1$

(D) $6 \times 6 \times 6$

7. Which lists all the factors of 27?

(A) 1, 2, 7

(B) 3, 9

(C) 1, 3, 9, 27

(D) 3, 9, 27, 54

8. Which is **not** a prime number?

(A) 17   (C) 35

(B) 23   (D) 47

9. What is 39,746 rounded to the nearest 1000?

(A) 40,000   (C) 39,700

(B) 39,000   (D) 39,800

10. Which number comes next?

4, 9, 20, 43, ___?___, . . .

(A) 60   (C) 90

(B) 86   (D) 92

11. Which is a multiple of 11?

(A) 120   (C) 144

(B) 132   (D) 151

12. Which number is greater than 5746 but less than 5984?

(A) 5712   (C) 5879

(B) 5738   (D) 5991

13. Which number could go in the box to make this sentence true?

$$^-22 < \square < 18$$

(A) 22   (C) $^-22$

(B) $^-44$ (D) $^-20$

14. The product of $^-12$ and $^-5$ is

(A) a fraction

(B) a negative integer

(C) a prime number

(D) a positive whole number

15. 7,000,000 can be expressed as

(A) 7^6 (C) (10×7^6)

(B) (7×10^6) (D) (70×10^6)

16. Which is the greatest common factor of 96 and 126?

(A) 6   (C) 21

(B) 9   (D) 32

PRACTICE 4 • Context Clues

SAMPLES

Directions: Read the sentences. Choose the word that best completes **both** sentences.

A. Sally brought her shoes to the _____ to be mended.

Mrs. Thorn baked a cherry _____ for dessert.

Ⓐ factory   Ⓒ pastry

Ⓑ cobbler   Ⓓ toddler

Directions: Read the sentences. Choose the word that best fits in the blank.

For his birthday, Tim received a year's ___(B)___ to his favorite magazine.

B. Ⓐ participation   Ⓒ vacation

Ⓑ refund   Ⓓ subscription

Tips and Reminders

- Think of the different meanings you know for each word. Watch out for words that fit one sentence but not the other.

- Read the whole paragraph first. Try each answer choice in the sentence to see which one sounds right.

PRACTICE

Directions: Read the sentences. Choose the word that best completes **both** sentences.

1. The president will _____ the nation at 7:00 P.M.

There was no return _____ on the package Jayne received.

Ⓐ label   Ⓒ address

Ⓑ charter   Ⓓ postage

2. Cassie had a _____ on her legs after walking through poison ivy.

The young man regretted his _____ decision to quit the basketball team.

Ⓐ muscle   Ⓒ rash

Ⓑ fatal   Ⓓ hasty

3. Every spring Mr. Gomez _____ the trees around his house.

Grandma eats _____ every morning.

(A) plants

(B) prunes

(C) muffins

(D) branches

4. The cashier counted the money in the cash _____.

Citizens must _____ to vote.

(A) register

(B) drawer

(C) elect

(D) object

5. The jury will likely _____ the defendant.

The _____ escaped from jail last night.

(A) excuse

(B) confront

(C) prisoner

(D) convict

6. Mr. Parsons owns several _____ of expensive stock.

Angelina always _____ her lunch with Roger.

(A) divides

(B) bonds

(C) portions

(D) shares

7. Mrs. Powell lost her _____ somewhere in the department store.

Some people _____ their lips when they are upset.

(A) pout

(B) shield

(C) luggage

(D) purse

8. Please _____ your check to the application.

Sugar has become a _____ of the American diet.

(A) sign

(B) staple

(C) bounty

(D) fasten

9. My sister and I _____ washing and drying the dishes.

John was an _____ captain for the team.

(A) accumulate   (C) alternate

(B) assistant   (D) objective

10. The recipe called for a teaspoon of _____.

The old man's _____ advice helped the young boy immensely.

(A) token

(B) vinegar

(C) sage

(D) salt

Directions: Read each paragraph. Then choose the word that best fits in each numbered blank.

Since the 1980s, many scientists have studied the problem of global warming, which is caused by the "greenhouse effect." Carbon dioxide from cars, factories, and other sources of __(11)__ is released into the air where it forms clouds, and these clouds trap heat near the earth's surface. As this heat warms the earth, temperatures will __(12)__, icebergs will melt, and the level of the oceans will rise. __(13)__ of many nations meet yearly to try to agree on ways to reduce carbon dioxide emissions before the __(14)__ gets any worse. __(15)__, different nations have their own views of the causes and effects of global warming, and these yearly meetings seldom lead to any actions that will have __(16)__ results.

---

11. (A) weariness
    (B) profit
    (C) basis
    (D) pollution

12. (A) enroll
    (B) increase
    (C) vow
    (D) obtain

13. (A) Attachments
    (B) Cabooses
    (C) Representatives
    (D) Hemispheres

14. (A) gadget
    (B) situation
    (C) imagery
    (D) fitness

15. (A) Unfortunately
    (B) Enthusiastically
    (C) Hopefully
    (D) Especially

16. (A) rightful
    (B) unreal
    (C) internal
    (D) positive

The All-American Soap Box Derby is an __(17)__ racing event held every August in Akron, Ohio. Motorless cars, built and driven by 11- to 15-year-olds, rely on __(18)__ to propel them down a long track. These cars were once made out of wooden soap boxes, but fiberglass is the most common __(19)__ material used today. The __(20)__ weight of the car, including the driver, cannot exceed 260 pounds.

17. Ⓐ extinct
    Ⓑ inventive
    Ⓒ annual
    Ⓓ experimental

18. Ⓐ persuasion
    Ⓑ gravity
    Ⓒ sunshine
    Ⓓ gasoline

19. Ⓐ construction
    Ⓑ perishable
    Ⓒ miscellaneous
    Ⓓ destructive

20. Ⓐ extensive
    Ⓑ maximum
    Ⓒ decreased
    Ⓓ victorious

Mr. Edwards is fairly easygoing and not usually prone to emotional __(21)__. However, when he discovered that his son had made several unauthorized __(22)__ from his checking account, Mr. Edwards lost his temper and grounded Louis for a month. Louis apologized for several minutes and asked his dad to __(23)__ his decision. He promised to repay the money in weekly __(24)__ of $5.00 or more until the entire amount was repaid. As a result, Mr. Edwards agreed to ground Louis for only one week.

21. Ⓐ sorrows
    Ⓑ trances
    Ⓒ outbursts
    Ⓓ jigsaws

22. Ⓐ deposits
    Ⓑ exertions
    Ⓒ grimaces
    Ⓓ withdrawals

23. Ⓐ reconsider
    Ⓑ defy
    Ⓒ execute
    Ⓓ presume

24. Ⓐ landings
    Ⓑ tracts
    Ⓒ installments
    Ⓓ premises

PRACTICE 5 • Grammar and Usage

Directions: Read the paragraph. The underlined parts may contain mistakes in word usage. Choose the best way to write each underlined part. If it contains no mistakes, choose answer D, "as it is."

SAMPLES

<u>me and Tyler</u> spotted some deer tracks in the snow. <u>We followed it</u> into the
  (A)   (B)
woods. The tracks led us to the <u>most smaller</u> thorn apple tree in a grove
                                    (C)
where the deer had stopped. We <u>never did see any</u> deer.
                                    (D)

A. In sentence A, <u>me and Tyler</u> is best written –

  Ⓐ Tyler and me
  Ⓑ Tyler and I
  Ⓒ I and Tyler
  Ⓓ as it is

B. In sentence B, <u>We followed it</u> is best written –

  Ⓐ We followed them
  Ⓑ We followed they
  Ⓒ We followed him
  Ⓓ as it is

C. In sentence C, <u>most smaller</u> is best written –

  Ⓐ more small
  Ⓑ smallerest
  Ⓒ smallest
  Ⓓ as it is

D. In sentence D, <u>never did see any</u> is best written –

  Ⓐ didn't never see any
  Ⓑ didn't not ever see any
  Ⓒ never saw no
  Ⓓ as it is

Tips and Reminders

- Try each answer choice in the sentence to see which one sounds right.

- Watch out for incorrect forms of words, such as *smallerest*.

PRACTICE

Directions: Read the paragraph about wood carving and answer questions 1–6.

> Wood carving is one of the <u>most old forms</u> of art and has been practiced in
> (1)
> many cultures. The Northwest Coast Indians, especially, are known for their
> (2)
> <u>finely carving skills</u>. Artisans of the Haida, Kwakiutl, and Tlingit tribes are
> (3)
> famous for <u>they totem poles</u>. These gigantic wooden sculptures <u>told often</u>
> (4)
> <u>stories</u>. Some totem poles were made to poke fun at people who <u>hadn't never</u>
> (5)
> <u>repaid a debt</u>. Others were erected to commemorate <u>an important event</u>.
> (6)

1. In sentence 1, <u>most old forms</u> is best written –

   (A) oldest forms

   (B) most oldest forms

   (C) most older forms

   (D) as it is

2. In sentence 2, <u>finely carving skills</u> is best written –

   (A) fine carving skills

   (B) finer carving skills

   (C) finest carving skills

   (D) as it is

3. In sentence 3, <u>they totem poles</u> is best written –

   (A) its totem poles

   (B) them totem poles

   (C) their totem poles

   (D) as it is

4. In sentence 4, <u>told often stories</u> is best written –

   (A) told stories often

   (B) stories often told

   (C) often told stories

   (D) as it is

5. In sentence 5, <u>hadn't never repaid a debt</u> is best written –

   (A) hadn't not repaid a debt

   (B) hadn't repaid a debt

   (C) hadn't not ever repaid a debt

   (D) as it is

6. In sentence 6, <u>an important event</u> is best written –

   (A) a important event

   (B) the important event

   (C) this important event

   (D) as it is

Directions: Read the paragraph below and answer questions 7–10.

>   Mrs. Adams announced to her family that she planned to run in a
> (1)
> marathon within a year. Her children were skeptical, but Mrs. Adams was
> (2)
> determined to <u>prove we all wrong</u>. After three months of training, she
> (3)
> competed in an 8-mile race and <u>ran faster</u> than most women her age.
>
> Encouraged, Mrs. Adams continued to <u>train rigorous</u>. <u>She ran her first</u>
> (4)   (5)
> <u>marathon and finished, six months later!</u> She crossed the finish line a little
> (6)
> more than an hour behind the first female finisher.

7. In sentence 2, <u>prove we all wrong</u> is best written –

   Ⓐ prove them all wrong

   Ⓑ prove they all wrong

   Ⓒ prove it all wrong

   Ⓓ as it is

8. In sentence 3, <u>ran faster</u> is best written –

   Ⓐ ran more fast

   Ⓑ ran fastest

   Ⓒ ran more fastly

   Ⓓ as it is

9. In sentence 4, <u>train rigorous</u> is best written –

   Ⓐ train more rigorous

   Ⓑ train rigorouser

   Ⓒ train rigorously

   Ⓓ as it is

10. How is sentence 5 best written?

   Ⓐ Six months later, Mrs. Adams ran her first marathon and finished!

   Ⓑ Mrs. Adams ran her marathon and finished first six months later!

   Ⓒ Mrs. Adams ran her first marathon and, six months later, finished!

   Ⓓ as it is

PRACTICE 6 • Fractions, Decimals, and Percents

Directions: Choose the best answer to each question.

SAMPLES

A. Which fraction is another name for $6\frac{1}{3}$?

Ⓐ $\frac{18}{3}$ Ⓒ $\frac{19}{3}$

Ⓑ $\frac{9}{3}$ Ⓓ $\frac{61}{3}$

B. What is 27.364 rounded to the nearest tenth?

Ⓐ 27.0   Ⓒ 27.37

Ⓑ 27.3   Ⓓ 27.4

Tips and Reminders

- To compare fractions, change them to "like" fractions with the same denominator.
- To compare decimal numbers, line up the decimal points.

PRACTICE

1. Which list shows the fractions in order from least to greatest?

Ⓐ $\frac{1}{9}, \frac{1}{6}, \frac{3}{4}, \frac{7}{8}$

Ⓑ $\frac{7}{11}, \frac{2}{3}, \frac{5}{9}, \frac{6}{13}$

Ⓒ $\frac{8}{9}, \frac{12}{17}, \frac{6}{7}, \frac{5}{8}$

Ⓓ $\frac{5}{12}, \frac{1}{2}, \frac{5}{6}, \frac{3}{4}$

2. What is 2.25 written as a fraction?

Ⓐ $2\frac{2}{25}$

Ⓑ $2\frac{1}{4}$

Ⓒ $\frac{225}{1000}$

Ⓓ $\frac{3}{4}$

3. What is 0.04 written as a percent?

Ⓐ 0.04%

Ⓑ 0.4%

Ⓒ 4%

Ⓓ 40%

4. Which number sentence is true?

Ⓐ 0.25 > 0.52

Ⓑ 0.78 = 0.078

Ⓒ 1.15 > 11.5

Ⓓ 0.37 < 0.39

5. What is 12.156 rounded to the nearest hundredth?

(A) 12.1   (C) 12.16

(B) 12.15   (D) 12.2

6. Which list shows the decimal numbers in order from least to greatest?

(A) 0.46, 0.046, 4.06, 4.60

(B) 4.06, 4.60, 0.046, 0.46

(C) 4.60, 4.06, 0.46, 0.046

(D) 0.046, 0.46, 4.06, 4.60

7. Which number sentence is true?

(A) $\frac{5}{8} < \frac{3}{4}$

(B) $\frac{13}{4} = \frac{27}{8}$

(C) $\frac{7}{20} > \frac{4}{10}$

(D) $1\frac{1}{3} = \frac{2}{3}$

8. What is $\frac{3}{8}$ written as a decimal number?

(A) 0.3   (C) 2.67

(B) 0.375   (D) 3.75

9. Which arrow points to a decimal number that is equivalent to $\frac{3}{4}$?

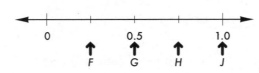

F   G   H   J

(A)   (B)   (C)   (D)

10. Which is 0.067 written as a percent?

(A) 670%   (C) 6.7%

(B) 67%   (D) 0.67%

11. Which fraction is another name for $2\frac{5}{12}$?

(A) $\frac{29}{12}$ (C) $\frac{24}{12}$

(B) $\frac{25}{12}$ (D) $\frac{19}{12}$

12. What is the value of the **9** in 4.2596?

(A) $\frac{9}{10}$

(B) $\frac{9}{100}$

(C) $\frac{9}{1000}$

(D) $\frac{9}{10,000}$

13. Which decimal number has the greatest value?

(A) 23.794

(B) 23.862

(C) 23.578

(D) 23.875

14. What is 45% written as a decimal number?

(A) 0.0045   (C) 0.45

(B) 0.045   (D) 4.50

15. What is $\frac{6}{15}$ expressed as a percent?

(A) 4%

(B) 40%

(C) 2.5%

(D) 25%

PRACTICE 7 • Word Analysis

SAMPLES

Directions: Read the sentence and the question. Choose the word that best answers the question.

A. Last year's harvest was _____.

Which word would suggest that the harvest was very large?

   Ⓐ adequate   Ⓒ ample

   Ⓑ bountiful   Ⓓ sufficient

Directions: Read the meaning of the original word. Then choose the modern word that comes from the original word.

B. Which word probably comes from the Old Norse word *skopa,* meaning "to jump or run"?

   Ⓐ scope   Ⓒ skin

   Ⓑ score   Ⓓ skip

Tips and Reminders

- The *connotation* of a word is the meaning that it suggests. To find the correct connotation, think about the suggested meaning of each word.

- To find the modern word that comes from an original word, look carefully at the spelling of each answer choice and think about what it means.

PRACTICE

Directions: Read the sentence and the question. Choose the word that best answers the question.

1. One _____ apple sat in the bowl.

Which word would suggest that the apple was very old and dry?

   Ⓐ shriveled   Ⓒ faded

   Ⓑ rotten   Ⓓ wilted

2. The cat _____ the canary.

Which word would suggest that the canary felt extreme fear?

   Ⓐ terrorized   Ⓒ alarmed

   Ⓑ startled   Ⓓ scared

3. David _____ a bone in his foot.

Which word suggests the least serious injury?

(A) bruised   (C) splintered

(B) fractured   (D) crushed

4. Everyone liked the cheese except Gwen, who thought the flavor was _____.

Which word suggests the strongest reaction on Gwen's part?

(A) disagreeable   (C) unpleasant

(B) distasteful   (D) repulsive

5. Dad's baseball cap was _____ with paint after he finished the porch ceiling.

Which word would suggest that the cap had just a few drops of paint on it?

(A) flecked   (C) spattered

(B) splattered   (D) covered

6. The old man _____ that the sleeping volcano would erupt soon.

Which word suggests a special and mysterious knowledge of the future?

(A) guessed   (C) stated

(B) prophesied   (D) estimated

7. Monte _____ avoided a collision with the other car.

Which word suggests a very close call?

(A) partly   (C) barely

(B) hardly   (D) surely

Directions: Read the meaning of the original word. Then choose the modern word that comes from the original word.

8. Which word probably comes from the Old English word *pudd,* meaning "ditch"?

(A) puddle   (C) pudgy

(B) pudding   (D) putty

9. Which word probably comes from the Old French word *grave,* meaning "coarse sand" or "seashore"?

(A) grove   (C) gravel

(B) gravity   (D) gravy

10. Which word probably comes from the Spanish *el legarto,* meaning "lizard"?

(A) alligator   (C) legend

(B) illegal   (D) legacy

11. Which word probably comes from the Latin word *quantus,* meaning "how much"?

(A) squander   (C) quarrel

(B) quantity   (D) quarry

12. Which word probably comes from the Old English word *writha,* meaning "something wound or coiled"?

(A) write   (C) wrap

(B) wrist   (D) wreath

PRACTICE 8 • Sentences

SAMPLES

Directions: Choose the simple subject of the sentence.

  A. A <u>red-haired</u> <u>girl</u> <u>dashed</u> <u>by</u>.
          Ⓐ   Ⓑ   Ⓒ   Ⓓ

Directions: Choose the simple predicate.

  B. <u>Max</u> <u>slowly</u> <u>climbed</u> the <u>stairs</u>.
      Ⓐ   Ⓑ   Ⓒ   Ⓓ

Directions: Find the answer that is a complete sentence written correctly.

  C. Ⓐ A huge crowd filled the arena.

       Ⓑ Skaters streamed onto the ice the crowd cheered.

       Ⓒ Standing to sing the national anthem.

       Ⓓ Scored a goal just two minutes into the first period of the game.

> **Tips and Reminders**
>
> - To find the subject of a sentence, ask yourself *who* or *what* is doing or did something ("A red-haired <u>girl</u> dashed . . .").
>
> - To find the predicate of a sentence, ask yourself *what* the person or thing is doing or did ("Max <u>climbed</u> . . .").
>
> - A complete sentence has a subject and a verb and expresses a complete thought. Watch out for answers that include two sentences run together.

PRACTICE

Directions: Choose the simple subject of the sentence.

  1. <u>My</u> <u>sister</u> <u>sighed</u> with relief when she read her school <u>report</u>.
     Ⓐ Ⓑ   Ⓒ   Ⓓ

  2. Off the <u>coast</u> of <u>Australia</u>, a <u>group</u> of American <u>divers</u> got caught in the storm.
                Ⓐ   Ⓑ   Ⓒ   Ⓓ

  3. <u>Eloise</u> <u>flipped</u> through the <u>channels</u> and then turned off the <u>TV</u>.
      Ⓐ   Ⓑ   Ⓒ   Ⓓ

4. A <u>dense</u> <u>yellow</u> <u>fog</u> blanketed the <u>harbor</u>.
   Ⓐ   Ⓑ   Ⓒ   Ⓓ

5. <u>Some</u> <u>frogs</u> <u>lay</u> tens of thousands of <u>eggs</u>.
   Ⓐ   Ⓑ   Ⓒ   Ⓓ

Directions: Choose the simple predicate of the sentence.

6. The <u>gardener</u> <u>carefully</u> <u>trimmed</u> the <u>shrubs</u> into ornamental shapes.
        Ⓐ   Ⓑ   Ⓒ   Ⓓ

7. <u>Several</u> <u>individuals</u> <u>spotted</u> <u>coyotes</u> in the canyon.
     Ⓐ   Ⓑ   Ⓒ   Ⓓ

8. <u>Luckily</u>, the <u>detergent</u> <u>easily</u> <u>eliminated</u> all traces of the chocolate!
     Ⓐ   Ⓑ   Ⓒ   Ⓓ

9. <u>There</u> <u>were</u> no <u>casualties</u> from the <u>car</u> accident.
     Ⓐ   Ⓑ   Ⓒ   Ⓓ

10. A <u>sinister</u> <u>figure</u> in a black <u>cape</u> <u>crept</u> onto the stage.
       Ⓐ   Ⓑ   Ⓒ   Ⓓ

Directions: Find the answer that is a complete sentence written correctly.

11. Ⓐ   Ireland, called the "Emerald Isle."
    Ⓑ   West winds blow across the island they bring 200 cm of rain each year.
    Ⓒ   Ireland has a long tradition of producing great poets and musicians.
    Ⓓ   A booming tourist industry as well as an electronics industry.

12. Ⓐ   An ominous sound in the night.
    Ⓑ   I woke up terrified I leaped out of bed.
    Ⓒ   Rushing to the window, I could see nothing unusual.
    Ⓓ   According to my mother, probably a screech owl.

13. Ⓐ Board games from many different time periods and places.

Ⓑ Many early games such as chess were based on battle strategies.

Ⓒ Playing board games as early as 4000 years ago!

Ⓓ Many board games involve dice one such game is Parcheesi™.

14. Ⓐ The shrew is a tiny animal it resembles a mouse.

Ⓑ With a longer nose and smaller body.

Ⓒ Shrews are adapted to hunting in the dark water shrews live on fish.

Ⓓ Each day, a shrew must eat food equivalent to its own body weight.

15. Ⓐ Em has a complex bedtime ritual.

Ⓑ Soaks her retainer in a cleaner.

Ⓒ Braids her hair so it doesn't tangle.

Ⓓ Last, she lays out her clothes for the next day arranges them on the chair.

16. Ⓐ Studying the life cycle of the turtle.

Ⓑ Baby turtles are born at the ocean's edge, and many die.

Ⓒ Predators such as gulls, crabs, and even human beings.

Ⓓ Scientists trying to learn how to protect the young turtles.

17. Ⓐ A severe shortage of rain in Connecticut last summer.

Ⓑ In many parts of the state, wells ran dry.

Ⓒ Lawns turned brown young trees lost their leaves early in the fall.

Ⓓ Luckily, torrential rains in September and October.

18. Ⓐ The periodicals room at the library.

Ⓑ Overstuffed chairs, pleasant lighting, and a quiet atmosphere.

Ⓒ Sarah inspected the magazines from all over the world.

Ⓓ Chose a fashion magazine from Italy.

19. Ⓐ The Maori people of New Zealand.

Ⓑ Traveled from Polynesia to New Zealand about 1000 years ago.

Ⓒ Living in peace and prosperity for nearly seven centuries.

Ⓓ Many Maoris still practice some of their traditional ways.

20. Ⓐ Mrs. Kovacs had three eggs, a zucchini, and a bit of cheese.

Ⓑ Trying to think of a good recipe.

Ⓒ Her daughter suggested an omelette there weren't enough eggs, though.

Ⓓ A zucchini and cheese pancake!

PRACTICE 9 • Number Operations

Directions: Choose the best answer to each question.

SAMPLES

A. If $6n - 3 = 27$, then $n =$

    Ⓐ 4   Ⓒ 6

    Ⓑ 5   Ⓓ 8

B. If $a \times b = 140$, then $140 \div b =$

    Ⓐ a

    Ⓑ $140 \div a$

    Ⓒ $a \div b$

    Ⓓ 1

C. What are the coordinates of point S?

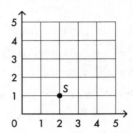

    Ⓐ $(1, 2)$ Ⓒ $(2, {}^-1)$

    Ⓑ $(2, 2)$ Ⓓ $(2, 1)$

Tips and Reminders

- Follow the order of operations carefully.

- Try each answer choice in the number sentence until you find the one that is correct.

- In an ordered pair, find the first number by counting to the left or right. The second number tells how many spaces to count up or down.

PRACTICE

1. $5(x + 4) =$

    Ⓐ $5x + 4$

    Ⓑ $5x + 1$

    Ⓒ $20x$

    Ⓓ $5x + 20$

2. If $8n \div 2 = 12$, then $n =$

    Ⓐ 2

    Ⓑ 3

    Ⓒ 4

    Ⓓ 6

3. If $a \times b = 48$ and $a < 6$, then

    Ⓐ $b > a$ Ⓒ $b < a$

    Ⓑ $b < 6$ Ⓓ $b = 6$

4. If $25x + y = 100$ and $x = 4$, then

    Ⓐ $y > 1$ Ⓒ $y \leq 1$

    Ⓑ $y < 0$ Ⓓ $y = 0$

5. If $4n - 3 < 25$, then

    Ⓐ $n \geq 7$

    Ⓑ $n < 7$

    Ⓒ $n > 7$

    Ⓓ $n = 7$

6. If $5b \div 4 \geq 10$, then

    Ⓐ $b < 8$

    Ⓑ $b = 8$

    Ⓒ $b > 8$

    Ⓓ $b \geq 8$

7. Which equation is true for all pairs of values x and y in the table?

x	y
2	5
3	8
4	11
5	14

    Ⓐ $2x + 1 = y$

    Ⓑ $4x - 7 = y$

    Ⓒ $3x - 1 = y$

    Ⓓ $x + \frac{1}{2}x = y$

8. If $n \div b = 6$, then which of these statements is true?

    Ⓐ $\frac{b}{6} = n$

    Ⓑ $6 \times b = n$

    Ⓒ $n < b$

    Ⓓ $\frac{6}{b} = n$

Use the grid below to answer 9–10.

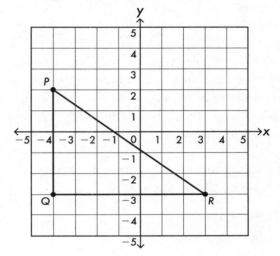

9. What are the coordinates of point R?

    Ⓐ (3, 3)   Ⓒ (3, ⁻2)

    Ⓑ (2, ⁻3)   Ⓓ (3, ⁻3)

10. What are the coordinates of point P?

    Ⓐ (⁻4, 2)   Ⓒ (⁻4, ⁻2)

    Ⓑ (4, ⁻2)   Ⓓ (4, 2)

PRACTICE 10 • Interpreting Text

Directions: Read each passage. Then answer the questions that follow.

SAMPLES

When Jason got home at 2:35, he began playing "Interplanetary Chess" on his computer. He had precisely forty-seven minutes of peace before his little brother Hunter got off the bus from elementary school.

Jason was working out a complex move when Hunter exploded into the house and yelled, "Hey, Jason, what are you doing?" When he swiveled around to answer sarcastically, "Snowboarding, of course," he hit the roof. Hunter had borrowed–without permission–Jason's favorite sweatshirt, which was about six sizes too large for his minuscule body. He had also spilled orange acrylic paint all down the front!

A. In the second paragraph, the word <u>minuscule</u> means –

  Ⓐ unhealthy

  Ⓑ naughty

  Ⓒ graceful

  Ⓓ tiny

B. The statement that Jason "hit the roof" means that he –

  Ⓐ leaped into the air

  Ⓑ became furious

  Ⓒ climbed up to the roof

  Ⓓ wondered what had happened

Tips and Reminders

- For words you don't know, look in the passage for clues that can help you guess their meaning.

- If a sentence doesn't seem to make sense the way it is written, look for a "hidden" or implied meaning. Use context clues to figure out what the sentence really means.

PRACTICE

There was trepidation in Meghan's voice when she told her mother she needed poster board for an assignment due the next day. Sure enough, her mother flew off the handle. They'd been to the office supply store just the previous afternoon, and after loading up on markers, binders, a mini-stapler and staple remover, and other supplies, Mrs. O'Neill had asked if there was anything else her daughter needed. Somehow, the poster for science class had completely slipped Meghan's mind.

Instead of whining or sulking, Meghan tried a new tactic. "Look, Mom," she said, trying to sound mature, "I know this is a pain for you, but I really need the right supplies to make a decent poster. But I'll pay you back—I promise! How about if I empty all the junk out of your car and vacuum it when we get back? It's really pretty dirty!" Mrs. O'Neill rolled her eyes, but she stopped harassing her daughter about the need to be more responsible and got her car keys. Meghan breathed a sigh of relief.

1. In the first paragraph, the word <u>trepidation</u> means –

   Ⓐ curiosity

   Ⓑ fear

   Ⓒ scorn

   Ⓓ boredom

2. Her mother "flew off the handle" means that she –

   Ⓐ rushed out

   Ⓑ got angry

   Ⓒ didn't hear

   Ⓓ fell down

3. The poster "completely slipped Meghan's mind" means that she –

   Ⓐ lost it

   Ⓑ didn't care about doing it

   Ⓒ forgot about it

   Ⓓ didn't understand how to do it

4. In the second paragraph, the word <u>harassing</u> means –

   Ⓐ bothering

   Ⓑ questioning

   Ⓒ quizzing

   Ⓓ embarrassing

Everybody loves a good cake. In Vienna, they really take their pastry seriously—especially the famous Sachertorte. The Sachertorte was created in 1832 by a baker named Franz Sacher. It is a delicious chocolate cake spread with apricot jam and covered with a rich chocolate glaze. Today, the bakery in the basement of the Hotel Sacher produces thousands of these confections each year. Only the Hotel Sacher may legally call its cake an "Original Sachertorte." Still, many other bakeries in Vienna turn out their own versions.

Austrians have a warm spot in their hearts, as well as in their stomachs, for the famous dessert. Viennese waltzes and ballets have been based on the Sachertorte. More devoted to the cake than any of his fellow citizens is master baker Friedrich Josef Pfliegler. For over 20 years, Pfliegler has kept watch over the bakery where each official Sachertorte is baked and assembled. His standards are high. Each cake that meets them is a flawless work of culinary art.

5. In the first paragraph, the word confections means –

   (A) performances
   (B) meals
   (C) chefs
   (D) desserts

6. Austrians have "a warm spot in their hearts" means that they have –

   (A) trouble digesting
   (B) fondness for
   (C) money to spend on
   (D) physical hunger

7. Pfliegler "has kept watch over" means that he has –

   (A) supervised
   (B) timed
   (C) owned
   (D) suspected

8. In the second paragraph, the word flawless means –

   (A) unknown
   (B) enormous
   (C) perfect
   (D) original

Language Arts

PRACTICE 11 • Punctuation

Directions: Choose the sentence that is written with correct punctuation.

SAMPLES

A.
- (A) Jess was listening to her favorite radio station, WLLL.
- (B) When she heard a barking dog she dashed to the phone.
- (C) The station was offering prizes such as CDs concert tickets and posters.
- (D) A voice on the other end said "Congratulations! You're a winner!"

B.
- (A) In 1929, disaster struck the United States financial market
- (B) Investors lost fortunes; and many companies were destroyed.
- (C) Banks shut their doors, private citizens lost their savings.
- (D) Elected in 1932, President Roosevelt helped put an end to the Depression.

> **Tips and Reminders**
> - Check every punctuation mark. Decide if the mark is needed, and make sure it is the right kind of punctuation.
> - Read the sentence to yourself to decide if it sounds right. If there is a pause in the sentence, there should be a punctuation mark.

PRACTICE

1.
- (A) Sidneys aunt lives in Baltimore Maryland.
- (B) Sidney's planning to take the train down to visit her next summer.
- (C) Sidney wants to see a ballgame but her aunt prefers the aquarium.
- (D) Is it true that Edgar Allen Poe lived in Baltimore.

2.
- (A) Fran's favorite poem is "The Dream Keeper" by Langston Hughes.
- (B) How striking it's simple images are!
- (C) The poem begins with the line, Bring me all of your dreams.
- (D) In addition to poems, Hughes wrote stories plays and articles.

3. (A) Over the course of history flags have had many functions.
   (B) Semaphore, a system involving flags, is used to spell out messages.
   (C) Before the radio was invented flags were used to send messages at sea.
   (D) Today; colored flags signal race-car drivers to slow down or stop.

4. (A) The telephone rang, and I raced to pick it up.
   (B) "Hello, Rosalia, said a familiar voice.
   (C) It was Mercedes my wacky aunt.
   (D) "Rosalia did I leave a frozen chicken in your driveway?" she asked.

5. (A) Jake couldnt find his silver medal.
   (B) He made a list of places to check; the car, his room, and the closet.
   (C) At his next swim meet, Mr. Malcarne handed him the familiar silver disk.
   (D) The coach explained "I found it beside the diving board!"

6. (A) Last year we visited London England.
   (B) After we saw St. Pauls Cathedral we went to the Tower of London.
   (C) I didnt enjoy the Tower.
   (D) The entry fee was too high, and the guides told gruesome stories.

7. (A) The dormouse which is a small rodent hibernates in the winter.
   (B) The dormouses heart beats less than once a minute during hibernation.
   (C) The black bear slows down in winter, but it doesn't truly hibernate.
   (D) The bear's temperature drops, but its heartbeat remains almost normal?

8. (A) Raymond's Run is a short story by Toni Cade Bambara.
   (B) It is told by Squeaky a young girl.
   (C) Squeakys brother Raymond is "not quite right" according to Squeaky.
   (D) However, Raymond also proves to be an accomplished runner.

9. (A) Mark Twain grew up in Hannibal, Missouri.
   (B) Anse my brother wanted to go there.
   (C) I didnt know you had relatives there!
   (D) Are you related to Mark Twain.

10. (A) Dear Dr Wu;
    (B) I am the president of the Young Womens Leadership Organization.
    (C) Id like to invite you to address our group.
    (D) We have meetings scheduled for these dates: November 18, March 3, and May 12.

PRACTICE 12 • Geometry

Directions: Choose the best answer to each question.

SAMPLES

A. The arrow points to what part of this figure?

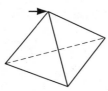

Ⓐ edge   Ⓒ vertex

Ⓑ plane   Ⓓ face

B. Which is an obtuse angle?

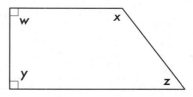

Ⓐ ∠w   Ⓒ ∠y

Ⓑ ∠x   Ⓓ ∠z

Tips and Reminders

- Look at the pictures for information. Draw your own picture if it will help you answer the question.

- After choosing an answer, read the question again to make sure you have answered it correctly.

PRACTICE

1. Lines *x* and *y* are parallel and are intersected by line *z.* Which angle is congruent to angle 2?

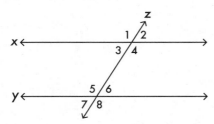

Ⓐ angle 1   Ⓒ angle 5

Ⓑ angle 4   Ⓓ angle 7

2. What is the circumference of this circle? (Use π = 3.14.)

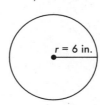

Ⓐ 18.84 in.

Ⓑ 37.68 in.

Ⓒ 75.36 in.

Ⓓ 113.04 in.

Use the figure below to answer questions 3–4.

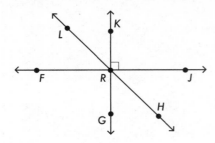

3. Which angle is formed by perpendicular lines?

  Ⓐ ∠GRH

  Ⓑ ∠HRJ

  Ⓒ ∠KRJ

  Ⓓ ∠LRK

4. $\overleftrightarrow{LH}$ bisects angle FRK. ∠LRF measures how many degrees?

  Ⓐ 180°

  Ⓑ 90°

  Ⓒ 60°

  Ⓓ 45°

5. What is the volume of this suitcase?

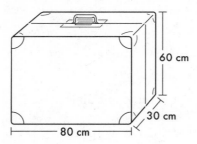

  Ⓐ 170 cm³

  Ⓑ 4800 cm³

  Ⓒ 14,400 cm³

  Ⓓ 144,000 cm³

6. What is the area of this rectangle?

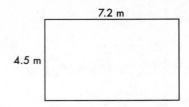

  Ⓐ 11.7 m²   Ⓒ 32.4 m²

  Ⓑ 18.9 m²   Ⓓ 64.8 m²

7. The two triangles below are similar. What is the length of $\overline{DF}$?

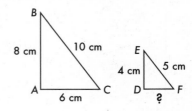

  Ⓐ 3 cm   Ⓒ 6 cm

  Ⓑ 4 cm   Ⓓ 7 cm

8. What is the circumference of a circle with a diameter of 15 in.? (Use π = 3.14.)

  Ⓐ 706.5 in.   Ⓒ 23.55 in.

  Ⓑ 47.1 in.   Ⓓ 18.14 in.

9. Which is an acute angle?

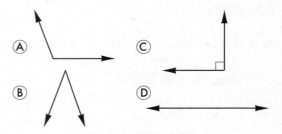

10. In an equilateral triangle, each angle measures –

Ⓐ 30° Ⓒ 60°

Ⓑ 45° Ⓓ 90°

11. What is the volume of this block of granite?

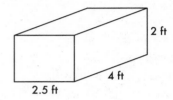

Ⓐ 8.5 ft³ Ⓒ 20 ft³

Ⓑ 10 ft³ Ⓓ 40 ft³

12. If triangle *PQR* is reflected across the *y*-axis, what will be the new coordinates of point *Q*?

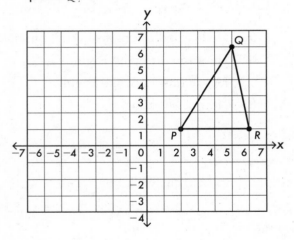

Ⓐ (⁻5, ⁻6)

Ⓑ (⁻5, 6)

Ⓒ (5, ⁻6)

Ⓓ (5, 6)

13. What is the area of this circular patio?
(Use π = 3.14.)

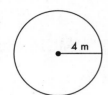

Ⓐ 100.48 m²

Ⓑ 50.24 m²

Ⓒ 25.12 m²

Ⓓ 12.56 m²

14. Which statement is true of triangle *XYZ*?

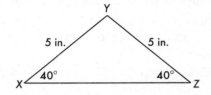

Ⓐ $\overline{XZ}$ = 5 in.

Ⓑ △*XYZ* is an equilateral triangle.

Ⓒ $\overline{XY}$ = $\overline{XZ}$

Ⓓ ∠*XYZ* = 100°

15. What is the diameter of this circle?

Ⓐ 21.25 mm

Ⓑ 42.5 mm

Ⓒ 85 mm

Ⓓ 133.45 mm

PRACTICE 13 • Main Idea and Details

SAMPLES

Directions: Read this passage. Then answer the questions below.

The Drama Department's spring production was going to be the musical *Oliver!* and Roger was going to audition for a part. Since Roger desperately hoped to play Fagin, he had learned "You've Got to Pick a Pocket or Two." Well, he hadn't exactly *learned* the song; it would be more accurate to say that he had practiced it over and over again. Despite his intense efforts, there were still a few lyrics that he stumbled over.

When he stood on the stage, blinking in the footlights and sweating, he tried to assume Fagin's wicked and jaunty expression, opened his mouth, and croaked, "Uhh!" He couldn't even remember how the song began.

A. Which is the best title for this passage?

- Ⓐ "Oliver!"
- Ⓑ "A Failed Attempt"
- Ⓒ "Playing Fagin"
- Ⓓ "The Drama Department"

B. Which detail supports the idea that Roger felt nervous about the audition?

- Ⓐ He learned a song from the musical.
- Ⓑ He wanted to play Fagin.
- Ⓒ He tried to look like Fagin.
- Ⓓ He was sweating.

Tips and Reminders

- Before you read, scan the questions quickly to see what you should look for in the passage.

- To find the main idea or best summary of a passage or paragraph, decide what the whole passage or paragraph is mostly about.

- Try to answer each question before looking at the answer choices. Check to see if your answer is one of the choices.

Go On

PRACTICE

Directions: Read this passage about asteroids. Then answer questions 1–3.

Our solar system is filled with pieces of rock known as asteroids. Sometimes one of them enters the earth's gravitational pull. Usually it burns up in the atmosphere, but sometimes a remnant hits the earth and causes great damage.

Today, scientists believe that there are about 2000 large asteroids following paths that could intersect the earth's orbit. If an asteroid smashes into the earth, the effect will be like many nuclear warheads exploding.

In 1997, the U.S. Congress approved money for a project called Clementine II. The plan was to learn more about asteroids and to practice eliminating them by shooting them with rockets. President Clinton vetoed the project, however, and it had to be shelved. Still, some astronomers are determined to continue studying asteroids, with or without government funding. They want to learn more about these potentially deadly objects before the next one hits the earth!

1. What is this passage mostly about?

   (A) the elements of our solar system

   (B) how Congress approves spending

   (C) the danger asteroids pose to the earth

   (D) how asteroids are formed

2. Which detail supports the fact that asteroids could be dangerous?

   (A) The impact of an asteroid could be like a nuclear explosion.

   (B) Asteroids burn up in our atmosphere.

   (C) President Clinton vetoed Clementine II.

   (D) Asteroids can be blown up in space by rockets.

3. Which is the best summary of this passage?

   (A) A project called Clementine II was intended to study asteroids and find ways to eliminate them.

   (B) Scientists believe there are about 2000 asteroids threatening Earth.

   (C) President Clinton vetoed Clementine II before it began.

   (D) Scientists are concerned about the dangers of asteroids, but research studies have been canceled.

Directions: Read this passage about giraffes. Then answer the questions below.

In the 1970s, Betty and Jock Leslie-Melville, an American writer and her Kenyan husband, bought a mansion in the highlands of Kenya. Both of them loved the wild animals of Africa and were devoted to conservation. When they learned that Kenya's last herd of Rothschild giraffes was in danger of becoming extinct, they adopted one of the seventeen-foot-tall creatures. Her name was Daisy, and she became the subject of a book and a movie.

Other giraffes later joined Daisy, and the Leslie-Melvilles' home was renamed Giraffe Manor. Today, up to seven giraffes roam freely over the Manor's 140 acres of protected land, and Betty's son has turned Giraffe Manor into a luxury hotel. Up to ten guests at a time can visit with the animals and even pet a giraffe's silky neck while drinking their morning coffee. Though a giraffe is strong enough to kill a lion, the mascots of Giraffe Manor are well-behaved.

4. What is this passage mostly about?

Ⓐ why Kenyan giraffes are in danger

Ⓑ a stay at Giraffe Manor

Ⓒ a movie made in Kenya

Ⓓ an unusual home for giraffes

5. Which detail supports the idea that the Leslie-Melvilles were devoted to conservation?

Ⓐ They moved to Africa.

Ⓑ They bought a mansion.

Ⓒ They adopted a giraffe.

Ⓓ They live in Kenya.

6. Which is the best summary of this passage?

Ⓐ The Leslie-Melvilles moved to Africa and turned their mansion into a home for giraffes.

Ⓑ Betty Leslie-Melville's son turned their home into a luxury hotel.

Ⓒ Guests can stay at Giraffe Manor and pet the giraffes.

Ⓓ Giraffes are strong and can be dangerous, but the animals at Giraffe Manor are quite well-behaved.

PRACTICE 14 • Capitalization

Directions: Read each passage and look at the underlined parts. If the underlined part has a mistake in capitalization, choose the answer that shows correct capitalization. If the underlined part is correct, choose answer D, "Correct as it is."

SAMPLES

(A)   Dancer Isadora Duncan was born in California in 1878. In 1896, she joined the <u>Augustin Daly Theater Company</u> in New York. Frustrated with traditional American dancing, she took her innovative new style to the

(B)   <u>countries of europe</u>.

A.   Ⓐ   Augustin Daly theater company
    Ⓑ   Augustin daly theater company
    Ⓒ   Augustin Daly Theater company
    Ⓓ   Correct as it is

B.   Ⓐ   Countries of Europe
    Ⓑ   Countries of europe
    Ⓒ   countries of Europe
    Ⓓ   Correct as it is

Tips and Reminders

- Check every word that has a capital letter. Decide if the word should be capitalized or not.

- Watch for words that are not capitalized but should be, such as the names of places and people and proper adjectives.

PRACTICE

(1)   Dinah's book report is due on <u>Friday, december 18</u>. She just finished

(2)   reading the novel <u>*A parcel of patterns*</u> by Jill Paton Walsh. This novel tells of what happened when the plague arrived in an English village.

1.   Ⓐ   friday, december 18
     Ⓑ   Friday, December 18
     Ⓒ   friday, December 18
     Ⓓ   Correct as it is

2.   Ⓐ   *A Parcel of Patterns*
     Ⓑ   *A parcel of Patterns*
     Ⓒ   *A Parcel Of Patterns*
     Ⓓ   Correct as it is

(3)   100 Kootenai Street
(4)   Boise, idaho
                                                                       May 12, 1998
(5)   dear mrs. Mahoney,
(6)   I am an eighth grader at Kelly Brook Junior High. As a member of the
           student council, I want to thank you for your generous donation to the
(7)   nichols library. I myself have already benefited directly from your gift. I used
(8)   an excellent british documentary film when gathering information for a term
(9)   paper on the design of new york's central park.

(10)   Yours truly,
                                                                       Rebecca Goldman

3. Ⓐ 100 kootenai street
   Ⓑ 100 kootenai Street
   Ⓒ 100 Kootenai street
   Ⓓ Correct as it is

4. Ⓐ Boise, Idaho
   Ⓑ boise, idaho
   Ⓒ boise, Idaho
   Ⓓ Correct as it is

5. Ⓐ Dear mrs. Mahoney
   Ⓑ Dear Mrs. Mahoney
   Ⓒ Dear mrs. mahoney
   Ⓓ Correct as it is

6. Ⓐ Kelly Brook junior high
   Ⓑ Kelly Brook Junior high
   Ⓒ Kelly brook junior high
   Ⓓ Correct as it is

7. Ⓐ Nichols Library
   Ⓑ Nichols library
   Ⓒ nichols Library
   Ⓓ Correct as it is

8. Ⓐ British Documentary film
   Ⓑ british Documentary film
   Ⓒ British documentary film
   Ⓓ Correct as it is

9. Ⓐ New York's central park
   Ⓑ New York's Central park
   Ⓒ New York's Central Park
   Ⓓ Correct as it is

10. Ⓐ Yours Truly
   Ⓑ yours truly
   Ⓒ yours Truly
   Ⓓ Correct as it is

PRACTICE 15 • Measurement

Directions: Choose the best answer to each question.

SAMPLES

A. In his first 3 tries at a video game, Marco scored 1200, 1550, and 2200 points. What was his average score per game?

- (A) 1550
- (B) 1650
- (C) 2475
- (D) 4950

B. The walkway through a park is 750 meters long. How many kilometers is that?

- (A) 0.75 km
- (B) 7.5 km
- (C) 75 km
- (D) 7500 km

> **Tips and Reminders**
> - Underline or jot down important information to answer each question.
> - Draw a picture if it will help you answer the question.
> - Make an estimate. Then try each answer choice. Rule out those that do not make sense.

PRACTICE

1. A football player ran 72 yards for a touchdown. How many feet did he run?

- (A) 288 ft
- (B) 216 ft
- (C) 144 ft
- (D) 24 ft

2. How many 8-ounce glasses can be poured from 1 gallon of iced tea?

- (A) 16
- (B) 24
- (C) 32
- (D) 128

3. At 6:00 P.M., the temperature was 4°F. If the temperature drops 2 degrees per hour, what will it be at midnight?

- (A) 16°F
- (B) 0°F
- (C) ⁻6°F
- (D) ⁻8°F

4. If the lamppost pictured below is 8 ft tall, what is the approximate height of the monument?

- (A) 20 ft
- (B) 30 ft
- (C) 40 ft
- (D) 50 ft

5. A dump truck moves 28,500 pounds of gravel. How many tons is that?

Ⓐ 14 T   Ⓒ 28 T

Ⓑ $14\frac{1}{4}$ T   Ⓓ $28\frac{1}{2}$ T

The table below shows the speeds of 5 race cars. Use the table to answer questions 6–7.

Car	Speed (mph)
A	182.5
B	178.0
C	190.2
D	188.0
E	185.3

6. What was the average speed of these cars?

Ⓐ 184.8 mph   Ⓒ 185.4 mph

Ⓑ 185.0 mph   Ⓓ 186.0 mph

7. What was the median speed?

Ⓐ 178.0 mph   Ⓒ 184.8 mph

Ⓑ 182.5 mph   Ⓓ 185.3 mph

8. What is the approximate mass of an 8th-grade social studies textbook?

Ⓐ 2 gm   Ⓒ 2 kg

Ⓑ 20 gm   Ⓓ 10 kg

9. Over 5 days, Clem read 65, 80, 72, 54, and 48 pages of a book. What was the average number of pages he read per day?

Ⓐ 62.5   Ⓒ 63.8

Ⓑ 62.7   Ⓓ 64.0

10. A bowl of mixed nuts holds 36 peanuts, 20 walnuts, 16 pecans, and 8 Brazil nuts. If you take one nut at random from the bowl, what is the probability of getting a pecan?

Ⓐ $\frac{1}{4}$ Ⓒ $\frac{1}{6}$

Ⓑ $\frac{1}{5}$ Ⓓ $\frac{1}{8}$

11. Miguel places 4 books on a shelf. In how many different ways can the 4 books be arranged?

Ⓐ 8   Ⓒ 24

Ⓑ 16   Ⓓ 32

12. If 4 girls and 4 boys pair up for a square dance, how many different pairs of 1 girl and 1 boy can be formed?

Ⓐ 20   Ⓒ 12

Ⓑ 16   Ⓓ 8

13. Pia rolls 2 number cubes numbered 1–6. What is the probability that she will roll a total of 7?

Ⓐ $\frac{1}{6}$ Ⓒ $\frac{5}{12}$

Ⓑ $\frac{1}{8}$ Ⓓ $\frac{5}{18}$

14. Charlene is making bracelets. She has 8 kinds of stones, 4 kinds of charms, and 4 kinds of chains. How many different combinations of 1 stone, 1 charm, and 1 chain can she make?

Ⓐ 32   Ⓒ 96

Ⓑ 64   Ⓓ 128

PRACTICE 16 • Text Structure

SAMPLES

Directions: Read this passage about grasshoppers and crickets. Then answer the questions below.

Grasshoppers and crickets belong to a group of insects called Orthoptera. Both have long back legs and ridged wings. Male grasshoppers and crickets are known for the chirping sound they make by rubbing their front wings together, or by rubbing a back leg against one of their wing veins. The sound is made to attract a mate or to warn rival males.

Grasshoppers eat only plants, but crickets are omnivores; they eat both meat and plants. Crickets have extremely long antennae, while grasshoppers have short antennae.

When a grasshopper or a cricket leaps, its bent hind legs straighten, and the insect's body is propelled up and forward, covering up to several feet in one jump. Sometimes when a cricket or grasshopper jumps, its wings open. Then the insect rises into the air and begins to fly.

A. Crickets are different from grasshoppers in that they

- Ⓐ have shorter antennae
- Ⓑ make a distinctive chirping sound
- Ⓒ have ridged wings
- Ⓓ eat meat as well as plants

B. Just before a grasshopper starts to fly, it

- Ⓐ jumps
- Ⓑ chirps
- Ⓒ rubs its wings together
- Ⓓ waves its antennae

C. A male grasshopper or cricket chirps when it wants to

- Ⓐ jump farther
- Ⓑ attack its prey
- Ⓒ attract females
- Ⓓ escape from a predator

Tips and Reminders

- Look for signal words in the passage to help find the sequence of events, causes and effects, or comparisons and contrasts.

- Read the passage carefully. Events may not be described in the order in which they occur.

PRACTICE

Directions: Read this passage about two students in Living Arts class. Then answer questions 1–8 on the following page.

Dan and Morgan finished mixing their mounds of pie dough and put them into the refrigerator to chill until the following day. Their school required that everyone take the six-week Living Arts course in eighth grade, and their teacher, Mrs. Mandelo, wanted her charges to make the most of their limited time in her kitchen.

"You have to respect her for that," said Dan. "But it was a little strange when she said if we were only going to learn how to cook one thing, it should be apple pie because we're Americans."

"I think she was making a joke," said Morgan.

The next day, Morgan listened intently as Mrs. Mandelo issued her Three Commandments of Crust: (1) Roll the dough in one direction. (2) Make sure the crust has an even thickness. (3) Do not over-handle the crust, or it will be tough. Dan absent-mindedly punched at his ball of dough while she spoke.

Fifteen minutes later, Morgan stared admiringly at his neat circle of crust. Dan was scrunching up his dough for a third assault; his crust kept sticking to the rolling pin as he pushed it rapidly back and forth.

By the time Dan was lining his pie pan with a lumpy layer of dough, Morgan had finished cutting his apples into thin slices and was sprinkling them with a cinnamon-sugar mixture. Dan chopped his apples into thick chunks, added a few spoonfuls of sugar, and then shook on some cinnamon.

"Okay, I'll bake these and we'll taste-test tomorrow!" said Mrs. Mandelo.

On Wednesday, pies of every shape covered the counters, and each one had a toothpick flag with the baker's name. Mrs. Mandelo passed around bite-sized chunks to evaluate. Everyone agreed that Morgan's piecrust was light and his apples were perfectly flavored. Dan's crust had a leathery toughness, and while some bits of apple were coated in sugar, others were bitter with too much cinnamon.

1. What did Mrs. Mandelo do first?

    Ⓐ She made a joke about apple pie.

    Ⓑ She announced the taste test.

    Ⓒ She critiqued the students' pies.

    Ⓓ She gave her Three Comandments of Crust.

2. Why did Dan and Morgan take Living Arts?

    Ⓐ They heard that Mrs. Mandelo was funny.

    Ⓑ Morgan had persuaded Dan that learning to cook would be fun.

    Ⓒ It was a required course.

    Ⓓ They signed up by accident.

3. By the time Dan started lining a pan with dough, Morgan was

    Ⓐ slicing apples

    Ⓑ cleaning the rolling pin

    Ⓒ conducting a taste test

    Ⓓ sprinkling cinnamon and sugar

4. What was the last thing Mrs. Mandelo did?

    Ⓐ baked the pies

    Ⓑ put a flag in each pie

    Ⓒ passed out bite-sized chunks

    Ⓓ took the pies out of the oven

5. Mrs. Mandelo wanted her students to make pies in Living Arts class in order to

    Ⓐ make the most of their limited time

    Ⓑ prove that they were Americans

    Ⓒ become trained for jobs as bakers

    Ⓓ understand the difficulties of baking

6. Why was Dan's crust so leathery?

    Ⓐ He chilled it too long.

    Ⓑ He rolled it too many times.

    Ⓒ He mixed the ingredients together.

    Ⓓ He baked it at the wrong temperature.

7. How is Morgan different from Dan?

    Ⓐ Morgan has no sense of humor.

    Ⓑ He is a better listener.

    Ⓒ Morgan is sloppier.

    Ⓓ He is always enthusiastic.

8. How was Morgan's pie different from Dan's?

    Ⓐ His crust was more uneven.

    Ⓑ His apple chunks were larger.

    Ⓒ His flavorings were better mixed.

    Ⓓ His pie had a flag attached.

Directions: Read this passage about operas and musicals. Then answer questions 9–12.

Operas and musical comedies are both stage productions that combine singing and acting. Operas, which began in Italy in the 1600s, are very formal, and almost every word is sung. Becoming an opera singer takes both great natural ability and years of special training. Among other things, an opera singer needs to project her or his voice to the back of a large theater.

In musical comedy, which grew up in the United States in the early 1900s, spoken dialogue alternates with song-and-dance routines. Musical comedy performers seldom have the long, formal training of opera stars, but they must be skilled in singing, acting, and dancing.

Audiences go to the opera to hear tragic tales of frustrated love, political intrigue, and revenge. At the end of an opera, the stage is often littered with bodies. At the end of Puccini's *Tosca,* for example, the heroine jumps off a castle wall after her beloved is executed. Earlier, she had been tormented by a tyrant named Scarpia and had killed him. Audiences who are looking for a laugh are better off going to musical comedies; most of them have happy endings.

9. How are musical comedies and operas alike?

   (A) Both combine singing and dancing.

   (B) Both originated in Italy.

   (C) Both use songs to tell a story.

   (D) Both require long, formal training.

10. How are musical comedies different from operas?

   (A) They have been around longer.

   (B) They use choruses as well as soloists.

   (C) They usually contain dance routines.

   (D) They often have sad endings.

11. In Puccini's opera *Tosca,* which event happens first?

   (A) Tosca's beloved is executed.

   (B) Scarpia torments Tosca.

   (C) Scarpia dies.

   (D) Tosca jumps off the battlement.

12. Opera stars must have years of specialized training to learn how to

   (A) project their voices

   (B) perform dance routines

   (C) appreciate opera

   (D) speak clearly

PRACTICE 17 • Spelling

Directions: Read each sentence. If one of the underlined words is misspelled, fill in the bubble under that word. If all the words are spelled correctly, fill in the bubble under answer D, "No mistake."

SAMPLES

A. The <u>villain</u> of the <u>novvel</u> is an evil <u>librarian</u>. <u>No mistake</u>
     Ⓐ   Ⓑ   Ⓒ   Ⓓ

B. The <u>rein</u> of the last <u>monarch</u> was <u>brief</u> and uneventful. <u>No mistake</u>
     Ⓐ   Ⓑ   Ⓒ   Ⓓ

Tips and Reminders

- Eliminate any answer choices you know are spelled correctly.
- Apply the spelling rules that you know.
- Check the spelling of any homophones (words that are pronounced the same but are spelled differently, such as *rein* and *reign*).
- If you are not sure which word is misspelled, look for an answer choice that looks wrong or that you have never seen before.

PRACTICE

1. Their <u>marriage</u> <u>ceremony</u> took place in a <u>hellicopter</u>. <u>No mistake</u>
     Ⓐ   Ⓑ   Ⓒ   Ⓓ

2. <u>Unfortunatly</u>, the letter contained some <u>errors</u> in <u>grammar</u>. <u>No mistake</u>
     Ⓐ   Ⓑ   Ⓒ   Ⓓ

3. Gilda <u>purchased</u> some <u>scented</u> <u>stationery</u>. <u>No mistake</u>
         Ⓐ   Ⓑ   Ⓒ   Ⓓ

4. Philip's <u>knowledge</u> of computer <u>programing</u> is <u>amazing</u>. <u>No mistake</u>
       Ⓐ   Ⓑ   Ⓒ   Ⓓ

5. Deborah took the <u>elevator</u> to the <u>eigth</u> floor of the <u>medical</u> building. <u>No mistake</u>
Ⓐ   Ⓑ   Ⓒ   Ⓓ

6. The <u>recipe</u> calls for <u>coarse</u> salt, rye <u>flour</u>, and yeast. <u>No mistake</u>
Ⓐ   Ⓑ   Ⓒ   Ⓓ

7. After finishing an <u>excellant</u> main dish, the <u>guests</u> enjoyed <u>dessert.</u> No mistake
Ⓐ   Ⓑ   Ⓒ   Ⓓ

8. The <u>senator</u> <u>designed</u> a new bill to protect the <u>enviroment</u>. <u>No mistake</u>
Ⓐ   Ⓑ   Ⓒ   Ⓓ

9. Kelly lives in a <u>development</u> quite <u>distant</u> from my <u>neighborhood</u>. <u>No mistake</u>
Ⓐ   Ⓑ   Ⓒ   Ⓓ

10. Before <u>beginning</u> his speech, the <u>acter</u> made a <u>horrible</u> face. <u>No mistake</u>
Ⓐ   Ⓑ   Ⓒ   Ⓓ

11. My brother <u>defeated</u> his <u>opponent</u> in the <u>wresling</u> match. <u>No mistake</u>
Ⓐ   Ⓑ   Ⓒ   Ⓓ

12. Mara made a <u>miniature</u> <u>palace</u> out of <u>sugar</u> cubes. <u>No mistake</u>
Ⓐ   Ⓑ   Ⓒ   Ⓓ

13. The <u>instructions</u> <u>omited</u> an <u>essential</u> step. <u>No mistake</u>
Ⓐ   Ⓑ   Ⓒ   Ⓓ

14. In Japan, a <u>bough</u> is a <u>customary</u> <u>greeting</u>. <u>No mistake</u>
Ⓐ   Ⓑ   Ⓒ   Ⓓ

15. Aunt Judith writes a <u>weekly</u> <u>colum</u> on <u>entertainment</u>. <u>No mistake</u>
Ⓐ   Ⓑ   Ⓒ   Ⓓ

PRACTICE 18 • Computation

Directions: Find the answer to each problem. If the correct answer is not given, fill in the bubble for N, "Not Given."

SAMPLES

A.   649
         + 73

   Ⓐ 712
   Ⓑ 720
   Ⓒ 722
   Ⓓ N

B. $3.2 \times 0.5 =$

   Ⓐ 3.7
   Ⓑ 1.6
   Ⓒ 0.16
   Ⓓ N

C. $2\frac{1}{3} - 1\frac{3}{4} =$

   Ⓐ $\frac{7}{12}$
   Ⓑ $\frac{2}{7}$
   Ⓒ $\frac{5}{12}$
   Ⓓ N

D. $11\overline{)255}$

   Ⓐ 22 R2
   Ⓑ 23
   Ⓒ 23 R5
   Ⓓ N

Tips and Reminders

- Look at the sign to see if you should add (+), subtract (–), multiply (×), or divide (÷ or $\overline{)}$).
- Always check your answer.
- When you work with fractions, be sure to simplify your answer.
- When using decimal numbers, check your answer carefully to make sure the decimal point is in the right place.

PRACTICE

1.   5836
         + 494

   Ⓐ 6330
   Ⓑ 6320
   Ⓒ 6220
   Ⓓ N

2.   4705
         – 2098

   Ⓐ 2507
   Ⓑ 2617
   Ⓒ 2717
   Ⓓ N

3. $83.20 − $71.90 =
- Ⓐ $12.30
- Ⓑ $11.70
- Ⓒ $11.30
- Ⓓ N

4. 35 × 2000 =
- Ⓐ 70,000
- Ⓑ 7000
- Ⓒ 700
- Ⓓ N

5. $3\frac{1}{4} \times 5 =$
- Ⓐ $4\frac{1}{2}$
- Ⓑ $15\frac{3}{4}$
- Ⓒ $16\frac{1}{2}$
- Ⓓ N

6. 99 ÷ 4.5 =
- Ⓐ 2 R9
- Ⓑ 20 R9
- Ⓒ 22
- Ⓓ N

7. 5.6 × 7 =
- Ⓐ 35.2
- Ⓑ 39.2
- Ⓒ 39.3
- Ⓓ N

8. $\frac{3}{5} \times \frac{5}{8} =$
- Ⓐ $\frac{8}{13}$
- Ⓑ $\frac{1}{5}$
- Ⓒ $\frac{3}{8}$
- Ⓓ N

9. $20 \div \frac{2}{3} =$
- Ⓐ 30
- Ⓑ $13\frac{1}{3}$
- Ⓒ 12
- Ⓓ N

10. $25.25
   × 8
- Ⓐ $200.60
- Ⓑ $204.00
- Ⓒ $204.60
- Ⓓ N

11. 12% of 80 =
- Ⓐ 6.67
- Ⓑ 9.6
- Ⓒ 12.8
- Ⓓ N

12. 0.09 × 0.04 =
- Ⓐ 0.0036
- Ⓑ 0.036
- Ⓒ 0.36
- Ⓓ N

13. 110% of $72.00 =
- Ⓐ $7.92
- Ⓑ $78.20
- Ⓒ $79.20
- Ⓓ N

14. 4.55
   0.82
   + 2.96
- Ⓐ 8.33
- Ⓑ 8.43
- Ⓒ 9.33
- Ⓓ N

15. $\frac{9}{10} - \frac{1}{3} =$
- Ⓐ $\frac{8}{7}$
- Ⓑ $\frac{17}{30}$
- Ⓒ $\frac{9}{13}$
- Ⓓ N

16. $\frac{3}{4} \times 15 =$
- Ⓐ $15\frac{3}{4}$
- Ⓑ $12\frac{1}{2}$
- Ⓒ $11\frac{3}{4}$
- Ⓓ N

17. 18 is equal to what percent of 90?

    Ⓐ 20
    Ⓑ 5
    Ⓒ 2
    Ⓓ N

18. $^-12 + 18 =$

    Ⓐ $^-30$
    Ⓑ 30
    Ⓒ 6
    Ⓓ N

19. $1.5 \times 0.723 =$

    Ⓐ 10.845
    Ⓑ 1.0845
    Ⓒ 0.10845
    Ⓓ N

20.
    259
     61
  1823
 + 77

    Ⓐ 2320
    Ⓑ 2120
    Ⓒ 2020
    Ⓓ N

21. $0.05 + 4.9 + 2.1 =$

    Ⓐ 7.05
    Ⓑ 7.15
    Ⓒ 7.5
    Ⓓ N

22. $^-32 - 15 =$

    Ⓐ 17
    Ⓑ $^-17$
    Ⓒ $^-47$
    Ⓓ N

23. $751 \div 8 =$

    Ⓐ 93
    Ⓑ 93 R7
    Ⓒ 93.78
    Ⓓ N

24. 42% of 800 =

    Ⓐ 19.05
    Ⓑ 33.6
    Ⓒ 336
    Ⓓ N

25. $9\frac{1}{8} \times 7 =$

    Ⓐ $62\frac{7}{8}$
    Ⓑ $63\frac{7}{8}$
    Ⓒ $64\frac{1}{8}$
    Ⓓ N

26. $4\frac{1}{2} + 2\frac{3}{5} =$

    Ⓐ $7\frac{1}{10}$
    Ⓑ $7\frac{1}{5}$
    Ⓒ $7\frac{2}{5}$
    Ⓓ N

27. $5.29 + 3.71 =$

    Ⓐ 8.90
    Ⓑ 8.89
    Ⓒ 8.80
    Ⓓ N

28. $\frac{2}{9} \times \frac{5}{6} =$

    Ⓐ $\frac{7}{54}$
    Ⓑ $\frac{5}{27}$
    Ⓒ $\frac{7}{15}$
    Ⓓ N

29. $\frac{2}{3} \div \frac{1}{7} =$

    Ⓐ $\frac{2}{21}$
    Ⓑ $4\frac{1}{3}$
    Ⓒ $4\frac{2}{3}$
    Ⓓ N

30. $^-9 \times {}^-30 =$

    Ⓐ $^-270$
    Ⓑ $^-39$
    Ⓒ 27
    Ⓓ N

PRACTICE 19 • Inferences

SAMPLES

Directions: Read this passage. Then answer the questions.

Supported by his father, Gustavo hobbled through the automatic doors and approached the front desk, where a friendly receptionist began to interrogate him. "Skateboard accident?" she asked sympathetically.

"No," muttered Gustavo.

"Then I'll bet you fell off your bike or got clobbered during a soccer game," she continued cheerfully.

"Not exactly," laughed Gustavo's dad.

"Dad!" exclaimed Gustavo, jerking his head toward the waiting area and its large TV screen. Gustavo took a chair, but his dad was still chatting with the receptionist. Gustavo realized that if he didn't distract him quickly, he'd tell her all about how his son had walked into a wall and twisted his ankle.

It was 7 P.M. Gustavo knew that his father's favorite hockey team was playing. He reached for the remote control.

A. Where is Gustavo?

- Ⓐ at school
- Ⓑ on a soccer field
- Ⓒ in a movie theater
- Ⓓ in a medical clinic

B. How does Gustavo feel?

- Ⓐ resentful that his father is so unconcerned about his injury
- Ⓑ embarrassed about how he got hurt
- Ⓒ fearful that the physicians are going to hurt him
- Ⓓ pleased by the receptionist's interest

C. What will Gustavo probably do next?

- Ⓐ turn on the TV
- Ⓑ yell at his father
- Ⓒ leave the building
- Ⓓ talk to the receptionist himself

Tips and Reminders

- To make inferences or predictions, look for clues in the passage.
- Check each answer choice to decide which is most likely.
- When you draw a conclusion, make sure that the information in the passage supports it.

PRACTICE

Directions: Read this passage about living and working in the United States. Then answer questions 1–4.

The United States of America started out as a country of farmers and small businesses. Then, in the 1800s, the growth of industry drew workers away from rural areas and towns. By the 1940s, more than half of all U.S. workers held manufacturing jobs. American cities were bustling centers of opportunity.

However, changes began to take place in the 1950s as technological advances made factories more efficient. By 1992, less than 18% of Americans had manufacturing jobs. A large number of factory workers were left stranded in the cities with neither the schooling nor the skills to find jobs in newly emerging fields. Cities became poorer and emptier as the better-educated professionals fled to the suburbs, which they viewed as safer, quieter, and richer in job opportunities. Housing developments, highways, and malls grew up in the suburbs to serve the growing population. Housing prices rose, and so did crime.

Today, computers and electronic mail have made it possible for many people to "telecommute" to work. As a result, they can do business almost anywhere. Suddenly, the rural areas and small towns are starting to look good again.

1. What happened as a result of the growth of industry during the 1800s?

   (A) Computers became obsolete.

   (B) Many people became farmers.

   (C) Shopping malls were built.

   (D) Many people moved to the cities.

2. You can conclude from this passage that most people are likely to choose where to live based on –

   (A) crime rates

   (B) farming

   (C) technology

   (D) job opportunities

3. Over the past few decades, the suburbs have become –

   (A) safer and quieter

   (B) more remote and isolated

   (C) more like cities

   (D) a refuge for the unemployed

4. Which of these changes is most likely to occur in the near future?

   (A) Most Americans will move back to the cities for factory jobs.

   (B) More professionals will move to rural areas.

   (C) Cities will become safer.

   (D) The number of farms will increase.

Directions: Read this passage about what happens to four friends. Then answer questions 5–10 on the next page.

As they entered the mall, Jenna dragged her friend Marisol into the Bath Shoppe to check out the scented soaps and lotions. A few minutes later, Jason and Jing-Chu came into the mall through the same entrance. Jason strode rapidly toward Keller's Music to pick up a CD. Jing-Chu stopped to watch a woman demonstrating model airplanes that swooped up and came back to her hand.

Inside the Bath Shoppe, Jenna was trying to distinguish among the twelve different scents she had applied to her left arm. Marisol, who was discovering a new allergy, was sneezing. Then she glimpsed Jing-Chu across the hall buying a model airplane. "I'll be outside!" she called to Jenna, whose nose was buried in the crook of her elbow.

"Dumb toy," said Marisol, "but I like your jacket. Is it new?"

"Yeah," answered Jing-Chu, "it has all these pockets and zippers, and it wasn't too expensive. I bet we wear about the same size."

A moment later, Jenna emerged from the fragrance shop, smelling like a garden and looking like a thundercloud. She scanned the crowd for Marisol's grubby yellow parka but couldn't spot it anywhere. So she headed down to Marisol's favorite clothing store, which was right next-door to Keller's Music.

Marisol returned Jing-Chu's jacket to him and saw a familiar figure flitting away. "Jenna," she trumpeted, but the din of the mall drowned out even her powerful voice. Marisol ran off after her friend, and Jing-Chu, who hadn't finished his description of his jacket, sprinted after Marisol.

Brandishing his CD, Jason burst out of Keller's Music and collided with Jenna, who bumped into Marisol, who was knocked over by Jing-Chu. Three small white bags holding a CD, a model airplane, and a bar of soap flew into the air, landed, and skittered across the floor.

After a short silence, all four friends groaned and accused everyone else of being at fault. They examined their heads, arms, and legs for bumps and bruises, then picked themselves up, still a bit shaky. Jenna, Jing-Chu, and Jason each saw a white paper bag lying nearby and picked it up.

5. Why didn't Jenna hear Marisol say where she was going?

   Ⓐ Marisol had a quiet voice.

   Ⓑ Jenna was preoccupied with smelling different scents.

   Ⓒ Jenna didn't care where Marisol was.

   Ⓓ Jenna was busy paying the saleswoman.

6. What kind of mood was Jenna in when she came out of the Bath Shoppe?

   Ⓐ angry because she didn't know where Marisol was

   Ⓑ pleased with her purchase

   Ⓒ jealous because Marisol was talking to Jing-Chu

   Ⓓ eager to locate Jason

7. Jenna didn't spot Marisol because Marisol was –

   Ⓐ back inside the Bath Shoppe

   Ⓑ trying on Jing-Chu's jacket

   Ⓒ inside her favorite clothing shop

   Ⓓ helping the saleswoman with her demonstration

8. Why did Marisol leave the Bath Shoppe?

   Ⓐ She liked Jing-Chu better than Jenna.

   Ⓑ She wanted one of the airplanes.

   Ⓒ She wanted to buy a CD.

   Ⓓ The smells were bothering her.

9. What can you conclude about the effect of the collisions on the four friends?

   Ⓐ Everybody was shaken, but no one was badly hurt.

   Ⓑ The girls were more seriously injured than the boys.

   Ⓒ Everybody had both bumps and bruises.

   Ⓓ Each of the friends thought the collision was his or her own fault.

10. What will probably happen next?

   Ⓐ The friends will throw the bags at each other.

   Ⓑ They will return their purchases.

   Ⓒ The friends will accidentally take the wrong bags.

   Ⓓ They will try out the model airplane.

PRACTICE 20 • Combining Sentences

SAMPLES

Directions: Read the underlined sentences. Choose the best way to combine them to form one sentence.

A. Farouk was juggling.

  Farouk was whistling a tune.

  Ⓐ Farouk was juggling and Farouk was whistling a tune.

  Ⓑ Farouk who was juggling was also whistling a tune.

  Ⓒ Farouk was juggling and whistling a tune.

  Ⓓ Farouk, he was juggling and whistling a tune.

Directions: Read the paragraph and answer the question that follows.

> Gary and Devon constructed a large water wheel for the science fair. Above the wheel, they suspended a bucket full of water. When the bucket was upended, water flowed over the wheel. The flowing water turned the wheel.

B. What is the best way to combine the last two sentences?

  Ⓐ When the bucket was upended, water flowed over the wheel and turned it.

  Ⓑ When the bucket was upended, it flowed over the turning wheel.

  Ⓒ When the bucket was upended, water turned the wheel and flowed.

  Ⓓ When the bucket was upended, water over the wheel it flowed and turned.

Tips and Reminders

• Check the order of words in the combined sentence to make sure it is correct.

• Make sure the combined sentence has the same meaning as the two original sentences.

• Be careful in using conjunctions. An incorrect conjunction can change the meaning of the sentence.

PRACTICE

Directions: Read the underlined sentences. Choose the best way to combine them to form one sentence.

1. Vincent hoped to win the match.

   Vincent was disappointed.

   (A) Vincent hoped to win the match, or Vincent was disappointed.

   (B) Vincent hoped to win the match, but he was disappointed.

   (C) A disappointed Vincent hoped to win the match.

   (D) Vincent, who hoped to win the match, he was disappointed.

2. Juncos visit our feeder.

   Wrens visit our feeder, too.

   (A) Juncos or wrens visit our feeder.

   (B) Juncos and wrens also visit our feeder.

   (C) Juncos and wrens visit our feeder.

   (D) Both juncos and wrens will visit.

3. Michaela has a tiny flashlight.

   She keeps the flashlight in her backpack.

   (A) Michaela, who is tiny, keeps a flashlight in her backpack.

   (B) Michaela has a tiny flashlight that she keeps in her backpack.

   (C) Michaela keeps her flashlight in her backpack, so it is tiny.

   (D) The flashlight which Michaela keeps in her backpack is a tiny flashlight.

4. Señor Cano is our Spanish teacher.

   Señor Cano is from Argentina.

   (A) Señor Cano teaches Spanish from Argentina.

   (B) Señor Cano is our Spanish teacher, so he is from Argentina.

   (C) Señor Cano, our Spanish teacher, is from Argentina.

   (D) Señor Cano is our Spanish teacher and he is also from Argentina.

5. A glow lit up the sky.

   The glow was reddish.

   (A) A reddish glow lit up the sky.

   (B) A glow lit up the reddish sky.

   (C) A glow lit the sky reddish.

   (D) A glow lit up the sky, and it was a reddish glow.

6. The pen leaked.

   The pen stained his shirt pocket.

   (A) The pen leaked and it also stained his shirt pocket, too.

   (B) Staining his shirt pocket, the pen leaked.

   (C) The pen leaked but stained his shirt pocket.

   (D) The pen leaked and stained his shirt pocket.

PRACTICE 20 • Combining Sentences (continued)

Directions: Read the paragraph. Then answer the questions that follow.

The *Amistad* carried African prisoners. The prisoners carried by the ship had been kidnapped from Sierra Leone. They had been sold into slavery and were being transported to a Caribbean island. One night, their leader freed himself from his chains and led a mutiny. The Africans tried to force their former captors to take them home, but the Spaniards tricked them and sailed to the United States instead. In the United States, a fierce controversy raged over whether to send the Africans to slavery in Cuba or to set them free. The Supreme Court eventually heard the case. The Supreme Court decided to free the prisoners.

7. Which is the best way to combine the first two sentences?

   Ⓐ The *Amistad* carried African prisoners they had been kidnapped from Sierra Leone.

   Ⓑ The *Amistad* carried African prisoners who had been kidnapped from Sierra Leone.

   Ⓒ The *Amistad* had prisoners from Africa and prisoners kidnapped from Sierra Leone.

   Ⓓ The *Amistad* had prisoners kidnapped from Africa, which is in Sierra Leone.

8. Which is the best way to combine the last two sentences?

   Ⓐ The Supreme Court eventually heard the case and decided to free the prisoners.

   Ⓑ The Supreme Court decided to hear the case and free the prisoners.

   Ⓒ When the Supreme Court heard the case, the prisoners decided to be free.

   Ⓓ Hearing the case, the Supreme Court decided to free the prisoners.

PRACTICE 21 • Estimation

Directions: Choose the best answer to each question.

SAMPLES

A. Which is the closest estimate of 589 ÷ 32?

- Ⓐ 500 ÷ 30
- Ⓑ 500 ÷ 50
- Ⓒ 600 ÷ 30
- Ⓓ 600 ÷ 40

B. The closest estimate of 5225 − 416 is −

- Ⓐ 5000
- Ⓑ 4800
- Ⓒ 4600
- Ⓓ 1100

Tips and Reminders
- To estimate, use rounding or estimating with compatible numbers.
- Use number sense to check your answer.

PRACTICE

1.

| 2 hockey sticks @ $31.25 each |
| 5 rolls tape @ $0.95 each |
| 1 pair laces @ $1.99 |

The total cost of all the items above is −

- Ⓐ less than $50.00
- Ⓑ between $50.00 and $60.00
- Ⓒ between $60.00 and $70.00
- Ⓓ more than $70.00

2. The closest estimate of 55,624 + 19,421 is −

- Ⓐ 800,000
- Ⓑ 80,000
- Ⓒ 8000
- Ⓓ 800

3. A fence panel is 2.4384 meters long. Which is the best estimate of the length of a fence with 8 panels?

- Ⓐ 20 m
- Ⓒ 14 m
- Ⓑ 16 m
- Ⓓ 12 m

4. The closest estimate of $72.49 × 5 is —

Ⓐ $450.00

Ⓑ $400.00

Ⓒ $350.00

Ⓓ $300.00

5. Which is the closest estimate of 7182 − 2546?

Ⓐ 5700

Ⓑ 5000

Ⓒ 4700

Ⓓ 4000

6. The closest estimate of 5582 ÷ 78 is between —

Ⓐ 60 and 70

Ⓑ 70 and 80

Ⓒ 80 and 90

Ⓓ 90 and 100

7. Which is the closest estimate of $0.23 × 50?

Ⓐ $200.00

Ⓑ $100.00

Ⓒ $20.00

Ⓓ $10.00

8. Which is the closest estimate of 103,652 + 646,324?

Ⓐ 700,000

Ⓑ 750,000

Ⓒ 800,000

Ⓓ 850,000

9.

White	Wheat	Oatmeal
284	139	96

Which numbers would give the closest estimate of the total number of loaves of bread?

Ⓐ 300 + 100 + 90

Ⓑ 290 + 140 + 100

Ⓒ 280 + 130 + 90

Ⓓ 280 + 140 + 100

10. Which is the closest estimate of 247,621 − 13,703?

Ⓐ 235,000

Ⓑ 230,000

Ⓒ 200,000

Ⓓ 23,000

11. 4808 ÷ 7 is between —

Ⓐ 60 and 70

Ⓑ 70 and 80

Ⓒ 600 and 700

Ⓓ 700 and 800

12. Which numbers would give the best estimate of $6\frac{2}{3} + 9\frac{7}{8} + 4\frac{1}{7}$?

Ⓐ 6 + 9 + 4

Ⓑ 7 + 10 + 5

Ⓒ 6 + 10 + 4

Ⓓ 7 + 10 + 4

PRACTICE 22 • Literary Elements

SAMPLES

Directions: Read this story about two giants. Then answer questions A and B.

Before the beginning of time, two temperamental giants roamed the world. Wherever they wandered, they kicked up tornadoes of dust, and their hats could obstruct the sun for days. Eventually, one of the giants decided that he was entitled to claim the entire world. So he sauntered up to his opponent and declared, "I want the whole world for myself. It's time for you to depart."

Outraged, the other giant shouted, "I've been thinking precisely the same thing. You must depart before sunrise." The first giant glowered. The second giant glared back and took a step toward his foe. The first giant lunged toward the second.

In no time, the two giants were tumbling and wrestling on the ground. They fought and they kicked and they poked and they gouged. They thrashed and they pushed and they flailed and they rolled. And as they did, they excavated huge ditches, and some of the dirt piled up and became the Rocky Mountains, some became the Andes, and some became the Himalayas.

The gouges became the Grand Canyon, the Atlantic Ocean, and the Dead Sea. And when the two giants were too exhausted to fight any more, they lay down—one at the North Pole and one at the South. There, they were buried under snow and ice, never to fight again.

A. This story would most likely be found in a collection of —

   Ⓐ history lessons

   Ⓑ legends

   Ⓒ science fiction stories

   Ⓓ fables

B. The theme of this story is most concerned with —

   Ⓐ why there are no more giants

   Ⓑ taking responsibility for your actions

   Ⓒ working together to solve problems

   Ⓓ getting along with other people

Tips and Reminders

- Look back at the passage to answer questions about details.
- For other questions, you may need to "read between the lines." Think about the story and what you already know to answer these questions.

PRACTICE

Directions: Read this story about a private detective. Then answer questions 1–8 on the next page.

"Dombrowski," the clerk said, "we hired you because we have a serious problem."

Dombrowski was standing in the warehouse of Goldie's, one of the largest auction houses in the country. Piled everywhere were hundreds of antiques–desks, letter openers, toys, chairs, diaries, vases, silver. The warehouse seemed crammed to the ceiling with enormously expensive, old, and dangerously fragile items.

"And the problem is?" asked Dombrowski, smiling helpfully. He was a private detective with an impressive mastery of U.S. history. His fee–steep by any standard–hadn't even raised an eyebrow at the Goldie's main office.

"The problem," said the clerk, "is that we have received an anonymous tip. One of these pieces, it seems, is a fake. A forgery. If Goldie's were to sell something that turned out to be phony, our reputation would be ruined. We'd be finished. Unfortunately, we don't know which piece is fake. All these items are due to be auctioned tomorrow, and we must find the counterfeit before it is sold. We want you to find it."

"I see," Dombrowski said. "Then perhaps I should begin." Dombrowski knew little about antiques. He looked at a Victorian cupboard; it seemed authentic enough. He looked at a gleaming silver picture frame; nothing seemed unusual. He looked at a threadbare stuffed bunny; it was clearly genuine.

He continued on for hours. A set of silverware–fine. A mahogany footstool–okay. Then he looked at a silver plate. It was hefty, but it felt soft; it was clearly real silver. It was bordered in a complex, dainty weave of silver ivy. That looked about right. It was etched very faintly on the bottom: "Mfd. by Peter Reynolds, Salem, Massachusetts, August 16, 1789." Dombrowski smiled. The auction was due to start in just two hours. He hailed the clerk. "I've found your forgery," he said, "and if you track down the source, I'm sure you'll find others."

The clerk looked at the plate. "Are you sure?" he asked. "This looks fine."

"It seems fine," Dombrowski said, "but it isn't. The date is wrong. The commonly used calendar back then was off by eleven days, so in 1789, it was adjusted to make it more accurate. At that time, eleven days were skipped. People went to bed on August 12 and woke up on August 23, so no one could have made this plate on August 16, 1789."

By the time the bidding started, the culprits were already in custody at the police station.

"We can't thank you enough," the clerk said to Dombrowski.

1. When does this story take place?

   Ⓐ during an auction
   Ⓑ in the 1700s
   Ⓒ during a meeting at the Goldie's office
   Ⓓ before an auction

2. The climax of the story occurs when –

   Ⓐ the culprits are taken into custody
   Ⓑ Dombrowski finds the forgery
   Ⓒ the calendar is adjusted for accuracy
   Ⓓ Goldie's receives an anonymous tip

3. Which words best describe Dombrowski?

   Ⓐ friendly but professional
   Ⓑ knowledgeable but unobservant
   Ⓒ bumbling but effective
   Ⓓ brusque and worried

4. How is the problem in this story resolved?

   Ⓐ The detective realizes that the silver plate cannot be authentic.
   Ⓑ The detective locates the culprits who made the forgery.
   Ⓒ The clerk hires the detective.
   Ⓓ The clerk lets the bidding begin.

5. How did the clerk feel at the end of the story?

   Ⓐ tense and anxious
   Ⓑ upset and angry
   Ⓒ relieved and grateful
   Ⓓ hopeful and confident

6. This story is an example of what kind of literature?

   Ⓐ mystery
   Ⓑ historical fiction
   Ⓒ science fiction
   Ⓓ fantasy

7. The mood of this story is best described as –

   Ⓐ suspenseful
   Ⓑ joyful
   Ⓒ oppressive
   Ⓓ scary

8. The author sets the tone of the story mainly in the fourth paragraph by –

   Ⓐ stating the detective's qualifications
   Ⓑ explaining the importance of the detective's success
   Ⓒ describing the setting of the story
   Ⓓ implying that the clerk has a problem

Directions: Read this story about Julia's vacation plans. Then answer questions 9–16.

Julia had never been to Puerto Rico before. When her parents announced that the family was going to visit her cousin Luis's family for a winter vacation, she decided to learn as much as she could about the island.

She already knew that it was warm there, even in winter, because her parents often reminisced about its climate. Although they said they did not want to move back, her parents never seemed to stop complaining about New York's weather, especially the snowstorms. The thought of warm, balmy evenings and sleeping on the porch of the hacienda was an enchanting vision. Julia could hardly wait to get there.

Puerto Rico is a relatively small island, and the water would be warm, salty, and inviting. Julia packed a bathing suit. Luis had described in his letters the great snorkeling that Puerto Rico offered—warm, shallow waters; bulging coral formations; brightly colored fish. She made a mental note to buy an inexpensive, disposable, underwater camera once she arrived; it would be great to show her friends at school pictures of the things she had seen in the sea.

Julia also learned that Puerto Rico was a United States territory. There were some people on the island who wanted it to become the fifty-first U.S. state and others who wanted Puerto Rico to be independent.

At last, the time came to head south. Julia's father drove the family to the airport, they all checked their luggage at the counter, and they headed for the gate. When a sudden draft sent chills down her spine, Julia thought, "That's the last time I'll feel that icy wind for a while."

On the plane, the flight attendants served the passengers a snack and told them about the flight. Then the head flight attendant took the microphone.

"I have a contest for passengers under 18 years old," she said. "I will give a prize to the first person who can show me a genuine piece of Puerto Rican currency."

Many of the young people on the plane looked puzzled. How could they have any money from a place they hadn't been to yet? Some of the children eyed their parents, requesting some help. But Julia beamed. She dug into her pocket and pulled out a crumpled U.S. dollar.

"We have a winner!" the flight attendant announced. "Because Puerto Rico is a U.S. territory, the currency is the same as in the United States!" She invited Julia to stand up. And then she produced the prize—a bright yellow, compact, disposable, underwater camera. The flight attendant smiled. "Enjoy your trip!" she said.

9. Which sentence best summarizes the plot of this story?

   (A) Julia wins a camera because she learned a lot about Puerto Rico.

   (B) Julia's family is going to visit her cousin Luis.

   (C) Julia has never been to Puerto Rico before.

   (D) Julia is eager to escape New York's cold winters.

10. Which word best describes the mood of this story?

   (A) suspense

   (B) anticipation

   (C) loneliness

   (D) nostalgia

11. Julia is best described as —

   (A) nervous and silly

   (B) bookish and antisocial

   (C) capable and industrious

   (D) uptight and dull

12. When did Julia's parents most likely live in Puerto Rico?

   (A) last winter

   (B) when Julia was a baby

   (C) before Julia was born

   (D) when Julia lived in her own apartment

13. What is the setting at the beginning of the story?

   (A) a beach

   (B) Puerto Rico

   (C) an airplane

   (D) New York City

14. What is the climax of this story?

   (A) Julia's family arrives in Puerto Rico.

   (B) Julia learns about life in Puerto Rico.

   (C) Julia wins a camera.

   (D) Julia's family plans a trip to Puerto Rico.

15. Which sentence from the story best indicates the narrative point of view?

   (A) "'I have a contest for passengers who are under 18 years old.'"

   (B) "Many of the young people on the plane looked puzzled."

   (C) "'That's the last time I'll feel that icy wind for a while.'"

   (D) "She already knew that it was warm there, even in winter."

16. How did Julia feel at the end of the story?

   (A) nervous

   (B) excited

   (C) afraid

   (D) tired

PRACTICE 23 • Composition

SAMPLES

Directions: Read this first draft of an article. Then answer questions A and B.

> Many people who live in cities long for the peace and well-being that comes
> **(1)**
> from working in a rooftop garden. Others seek the economic opportunities
> **(2)**
> that an intensively farmed garden offers. Children can grow carrots and
> **(3)**
> radishes from seeds. Whatever the goal, care must be taken to make sure the
> **(4)**
> roof is properly prepared to withstand the weight and traffic. New
> **(5)**
> adaptations such as lightweight soil substitutes and mini-drip hoses make
>
> rooftop gardens ever more feasible.

A. Which topic sentence would best begin this paragraph?

- Ⓐ Plants provide much needed fresh air for city dwellers.
- Ⓑ New technology is making it possible to put plants on rooftops.
- Ⓒ Plants are an important source of food for people who live in cities.
- Ⓓ Some city dwellers are building rooftop gardens for personal and economic reasons.

B. Which sentence does **not** belong in this article?

- Ⓐ sentence 1
- Ⓑ sentence 2
- Ⓒ sentence 3
- Ⓓ sentence 4

Tips and Reminders

- The topic sentence should tell what the whole paragraph is mostly about. Every sentence in that paragraph should support the topic.

- To determine the writer's purpose or audience in writing a passage, think about what the writer is trying to say and to whom.

- When revising a sentence, choose the answer that has the same meaning as the original sentence.

PRACTICE

Directions: Read this first draft of a report on uakari monkeys. Then answer questions 1–2.

Rare uakari monkeys live high in the treetops of forests along the Amazon River. Bearded sakis also live in the upper canopy of the forests. The uakaris' faces get flushed when they are excited, and they have nearly bald heads. In contrast, their fur is long and shaggy. Although most monkeys that live high in the treetops have long tails to help them balance, the uakari have short tails. In fact, they are the only short-tailed American monkeys.

Fish gather under the trees where the uakari eat to gather the scraps of fruit that fall into the water. The fish are then easier to catch. Sometimes, when the uakari are not around, the fishermen try to trick the fish by hitting the water with their paddles.

1. Which sentence does **not** belong in the first paragraph?

   Ⓐ Rare uakari monkeys live high in the treetops of forests along the Amazon River.

   Ⓑ Bearded sakis also live in the upper canopy of the forests.

   Ⓒ In contrast, their fur is long and shaggy.

   Ⓓ In fact, they are the only short-tailed American monkeys.

2. Which is the best topic sentence for the second paragraph?

   Ⓐ The uakari eat nuts, fruit, and vegetation.

   Ⓑ When eating fruit, the uakari are helpful to fishermen on the Amazon.

   Ⓒ Some people think the uakari look like people because of their bald heads.

   Ⓓ Fish have trouble finding enough food.

Directions: Read this first draft of a report on Edward S. Curtis. Then answer questions 3–8 on the next page.

He took more than 40,000 photographs of Native Americans from more than 80
 (1)
tribes. His specialty was photographs of people wearing traditional dress.
        (2)
Between 1907 and 1930, Curtis published a work called *The North American*
 (3)
Indian, which consisted of more than 20 volumes of text and 20 portfolios of his

photographs. About 300 copies were printed, but probably fewer than half of
                  (4)
them remain intact.

   Edward Curtis approached his work as an artist, not a scholar. He posed his
    (5)   (6)
subjects. Because he grew up in poverty, he had little schooling. Academics
          (7)   (8)
criticized his work because he did not have formal training. The Native
                                                        (9)
Americans with whom he worked, however, seemed to appreciate his sincerity

and trusted him.

   Curtis was dedicated to documenting the lives of Native Americans. In
    (10)   (11)
addition to taking photographs, Curtis was collecting stories, compiled more

than 10,000 recordings, and was making a film. He constantly faced difficulty
                                                  (12)
raising the money he needed for his projects, but he was a hard worker and

devoted himself to his passion. Often away from home for months at a time, his
                                (13)
wife struggled to take care of their children. Eventually, the marriage ended in
                                               (14)
divorce.

   At the time of his death in 1954, Curtis's work was largely forgotten. In 1951,
    (15)   (16)
Curtis had a portrait taken of himself. In the 1970s, his photographs began to be
                                          (17)
reprinted. Today, his photographs are valued as art and as ethnographic
            (18)
documents.

3. Which is the best topic sentence for the first paragraph of this report?

(A) His father brought home a camera lens from the Civil War.

(B) Edward S. Curtis spent more than 30 years traveling and taking photographs throughout North America.

(C) Edward S. Curtis hoped to escape the poverty of his childhood.

(D) Edward S. Curtis was an artist.

4. Which sentence could best be added to the second paragraph after sentence 6?

(A) He loved to listen to the stories of the people he photographed.

(B) He rarely had any leisure time.

(C) He also manipulated the images to create the effects he desired.

(D) He also liked to climb mountains.

5. Which is the best way to rewrite sentence 11?

(A) In addition to taking photographs, Curtis collected stories, compiled more than 10,000 recordings, and made a film.

(B) In addition to taking photographs, Curtis was collecting stories, recordings, and film.

(C) In addition to taking photographs, Curtis collected stories, compiled more than 10,000 recordings, and was making a film.

(D) In addition to taking photographs, Curtis was collecting stories, was compiling more than 10,000 recordings, and made a film.

6. The writer's main purpose in this report is to —

(A) compare Curtis to people with more academic training

(B) explain the relationship Edward Curtis had with his family

(C) describe Edward Curtis's life

(D) persuade readers to become great photographers

7. Which sentence does **not** belong in the last paragraph?

(A) At the time of his death in 1954, Curtis's work was largely forgotten.

(B) In 1951, Curtis had a portrait taken of himself.

(C) In the 1970s, his photographs began to be reprinted.

(D) Today, Curtis's photographs are valued as works of art and as ethnographic documentation.

8. Which is the best way to revise sentence 13?

(A) Away from home for months at a time, his wife often struggled to take care of their children.

(B) Often his wife struggled to take care of their children, who were away from home for months at a time.

(C) His wife, who was often away from home for months at a time, struggled to take care of their children.

(D) Because he was often away from home for months at a time, his wife struggled to care for their children.

Directions: Read this first draft of a report on netiquette. Then answer questions 9–10.

"Netiquette" is a combination of the words "etiquette" and "Internet." It refers to the codes of proper behavior when online. For example, when sending e-mail, it is considered rude to shout at your reader. People interpret writing in all capital letters as shouting. Occasional use of capital letters is okay, but don't overdo it. To soften your tone, you can insert a smiley face. :-)

Avoid sending "flames," which are messages intended to make other people upset or angry. No one needs a flame war.

Regular users of the Internet, or "netizens," can shape what kind of environment it offers. Each netizen has to decide how much shouting and how many smiley faces he or she is going to use.

---

9. Which would be the best topic sentence to begin this report?

(A) Lots of people use computers now.

(B) "Etiquette" comes from the French word for ticket.

(C) Recently, a new term was created to describe behavior on the Internet.

(D) No one knows how many people use the Internet.

10. The writer probably wrote this article for people who –

(A) have been netizens for years

(B) do not have access to a computer

(C) type in all capital letters

(D) have just begun to use the Internet

PRACTICE 24 • Interpreting Data

SAMPLES

Directions: Miguel wants to open a bank account. Use the table below to answer questions A and B.

Milton Bank Accounts	
Type of Account	**Interest Rate**
Checking	2.5%
NOW	2.6%
Savings	3.1%
Money Market	4.2%

A. Which type of account has the highest interest rate?

Ⓐ Checking   Ⓒ Savings

Ⓑ NOW   Ⓓ Money Market

B. What is the interest rate for a NOW account?

Ⓐ 2.5%   Ⓒ 3.1%

Ⓑ 2.6%   Ⓓ 4.2%

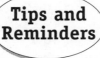

Tips and Reminders

- Use the graph or chart to find the answer to each question.

- After choosing an answer, read the question again to make sure you have answered it correctly.

PRACTICE

Directions: Susan has kept track of the daily high temperatures for five days. Use her graph to answer questions 1–2.

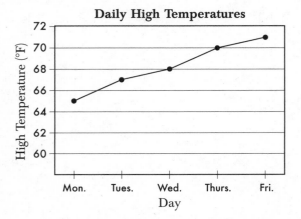

1. What was the high temperature on Wednesday?

Ⓐ 65°F   Ⓒ 67°F

Ⓑ 66°F   Ⓓ 68°F

2. If the trend on this graph continues, what will likely be the high temperature on Saturday?

Ⓐ 68°F   Ⓒ 73°F

Ⓑ 70°F   Ⓓ 77°F

Directions: This table shows car rental rates. Use the table to answer questions 3–5.

Car Rental Rates

Type of Car	Daily Charge ($)	Mileage Rate ($ per mile)
Compact	23.25	0.15
Sports	24.75	0.18
Mid-size	26.50	0.20
Full-size	30.25	0.24

3. Which car is least expensive to rent?

- (A) Compact
- (B) Sports
- (C) Mid-size
- (D) Full-size

4. What is the daily charge to rent a Mid-size car?

- (A) $23.25
- (B) $24.75
- (C) $26.50
- (D) $30.25

5. Compared with the mileage rate for a Sports car, how much higher is the rate for a Full-size car?

- (A) $0.24/mile
- (B) $0.18/mile
- (C) $0.09/mile
- (D) $0.06/mile

Directions: The graph below shows two stores' profits during a 5-year period. Use the graph to answer questions 6–8.

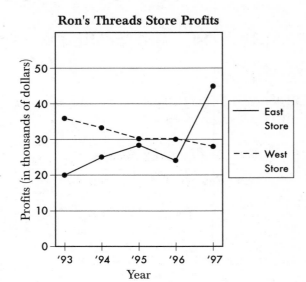

Ron's Threads Store Profits

6. In what year did the East store have its highest profits?

- (A) 1994
- (C) 1996
- (B) 1995
- (D) 1997

7. What were the total profits for both stores in 1996?

- (A) $24,000
- (C) $54,000
- (B) $30,000
- (D) $62,000

8. In what year was the profit of both stores about the same?

- (A) 1994
- (C) 1996
- (B) 1995
- (D) 1997

PRACTICE 24 • Interpreting Data (continued)

Directions: Use the graph to answer 9–11.

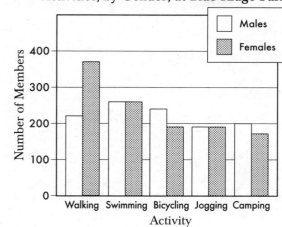

Participation in the 5 Most Popular Activities, by Gender, at Blue Ridge Park

9. Which activity is preferred by more women than men?

   Ⓐ walking   Ⓒ bicycling

   Ⓑ swimming   Ⓓ jogging

10. About how many more men than women participate in camping at the park?

    Ⓐ 3   Ⓒ 200

    Ⓑ 30   Ⓓ 370

11. About how many men and women combined participate in bicycling?

    Ⓐ 370   Ⓒ 410

    Ⓑ 390   Ⓓ 430

Directions: This graph shows the results of a survey of TV equipment in families' homes. Use the graph to answer 12–14.

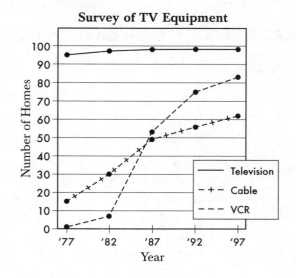

Survey of TV Equipment

12. In 1977, what percentage of families had VCRs?

    Ⓐ 1%   Ⓒ 15%

    Ⓑ 10%   Ⓓ 83%

13. What can you conclude about televisions from the results of the survey?

    Ⓐ More homes had VCRs than TVs.

    Ⓑ TVs became popular in the 1980s.

    Ⓒ Many homes did not have TVs in 1972.

    Ⓓ Most homes had TVs before 1977.

14. More than half of the homes surveyed first got cable service in the –

    Ⓐ late 1970s   Ⓒ late 1980s

    Ⓑ early 1980s   Ⓓ late 1990s

PRACTICE 25 • Evaluating Information

SAMPLES

Directions: Read this advertisement. Then answer questions A and B.

Why have the same old boring kind of party? For your birthday, graduation, or family reunion, order our knit shirts embroidered with your own emblem, picture, or message. Embroidered shirts for everyone in the group will make your next party a special one. You'll be the most popular person in town. They'll talk about your one-of-a-kind party for years to come. This week only, our special embroidered polo shirts are on sale for $35.00 each. So, get with the program, and call us today!

A. Which sentence states a fact?

  (A) Embroidered shirts will make your next party a special one.

  (B) You'll be the most popular person in town.

  (C) They'll talk about your one-of-a-kind party for years to come.

  (D) This week only, our special shirts are on sale for $35.00 each.

B. This ad tries to appeal to a consumer's desire to –

  (A) save money

  (B) be popular

  (C) buy high-quality clothing

  (D) be amused

Tips and Reminders

- A fact is a statement that can be proven true. An opinion is a statement, belief, or feeling that cannot be proven true.

- For questions about techniques of persuasion, think carefully about what the author is trying to say. Look for statements or claims made without any supporting evidence.

- When making a generalization, look for three or more details in the passage that support the generalization.

PRACTICE

Directions: Read this editorial. Then answer questions 1–3.

To the Editor:

Everyone knows that Americans are overweight, and it's high time we do something about it. The government has invented fitness programs and food pyramids. We have tried special diets and exercise videos. The doctors tell us that poor diet can cause heart problems. But none of these gimmicks has worked, and no one listens to the experts.

In this country, one in every five children and one in every three adults is overweight. Well, there's only one way to solve this problem: a junk food tax. People eat too much junk food. The only way to change their habits is to make junk food too expensive to buy. If we triple or quadruple the price of soft drinks, candy, and all sorts of other junk food items, people will stop buying them. Before they know it, they'll be losing weight and saving money.

Don't you think we ought to try this idea, while we can still get off the couch?

Dave "Slim" Ingster
Toledo, Ohio

1. Which sentence states an opinion?

   Ⓐ The government has invented fitness programs and food pyramids.

   Ⓑ The doctors tell us that poor diet can cause heart problems.

   Ⓒ One in every three adults is overweight.

   Ⓓ People eat too much junk food.

2. Which sentence states an unsupported generalization?

   Ⓐ Everyone knows that Americans are overweight.

   Ⓑ It's high time we do something about it.

   Ⓒ Well, there's only one way to solve this problem.

   Ⓓ They'll be losing weight and saving money.

3. The writer tries to convince readers to support a junk food tax because –

   Ⓐ it will raise money for education

   Ⓑ too many Americans are overweight

   Ⓒ exercise videos are too expensive

   Ⓓ Americans care more about money than food

Directions: Read this advertisement. Then answer questions 4–7.

> Have you worked hard all your life to buy a piece of the American dream? Are you tired of lazy neighbors who don't cut their lawns? Do you worry about the high crime rate in almost every neighborhood in America? Maybe it's time to move.
>
> Pheasant Run is a quiet, elegant, secure community for people like you. We have brand-new townhouses and condominiums available starting at just $280,000 for a one-bedroom unit. Each home is beautifully appointed and architect-designed. Our private security force keeps our streets safe. And a low monthly maintenance fee ensures that every lawn is cut and manicured. Real Americans value the elegance and safety we can offer. Isn't it about time for you to share the American dream that you know you deserve? Call us today at 555-1800.

4. Which sentence states an opinion?

   A Have you worked hard all your life?

   B Do you worry about the high crime rate?

   C Each home is beautifully appointed.

   D Each home is designed by an architect.

5. This ad tries to convince readers to buy homes at Pheasant Run by –

   A appealing to snobs

   B offering low prices

   C appealing to plain folks

   D offering testimonials

6. Which sentence states a generalization?

   A Pheasant Run is a quiet, elegant, secure community.

   B Townhouses and condominiums are available at just $280,000.

   C Our private security force keeps our streets safe.

   D Real Americans value elegance and safety.

7. This ad implies that –

   A the American dream is free

   B everyone deserves a nice home

   C most neighborhoods are unpleasant and unsafe

   D the homes at Pheasant Run are inexpensive and all the same

Directions: Read this editorial. Then answer questions 8–10.

Tallahassee is a fine town, but it should not be the state capital of Florida. An ideal state capital would be centrally located and easily accessible to people living anywhere in the state. It should have a good transportation system and excellent city services. As much as I like Tallahassee, it does not fit these criteria.

Perhaps you have already guessed where I think the state capital should be. That's right: Orlando, the greatest little city in America. The people of Orlando are the nicest people in the world.

Orlando has it all: great entertainment and recreation, an international airport and new highways. We have a world-class basketball team, while Tallahassee has none. We are close to the ocean and, unlike Tallahassee, Orlando is centrally located. If you live in Miami, for example, you can drive here in about four hours. Or you could drive to Tallahassee in about twelve hours.

There is nothing in our state constitution that says we can't change the site of the capital, and I say now is the time. Let's move the capital to Orlando and make Florida a better place.

8. Which sentence states an opinion?

   (A) Tallahassee is a fine town.

   (B) Orlando is centrally located.

   (C) If you live in Miami, you can drive here in about four hours.

   (D) Orlando has an international airport.

9. Which statement from the editorial is a generalization?

   (A) Perhaps you have already guessed where I think the state capital should be.

   (B) The people of Orlando are the nicest people in the world.

   (C) We have a world-class basketball team, while Tallahassee has none.

   (D) There's nothing in the state constitution that says we can't change the site of the capital.

10. The writer tries to convince readers to move the capital to Orlando by –

    (A) criticizing Miami

    (B) appealing to snobs

    (C) comparing it with Tallahassee

    (D) stating that everyone agrees this would be best

Language Arts

PRACTICE 26 • Study Skills

SAMPLES

Directions: Use this table of contents from a book on art history to answer questions A and B.

CONTENTS

Chapter		Page
1	Prehistoric Art	3
2	Stories in Cloth	31
3	Stories in Clay	55
4	Stories on Walls	78
5	Book Illustrations	91
6	Modern Art	115

A. Which chapter most likely has information about sculpture and pottery?

- (A) Chapter 2
- (B) Chapter 3
- (C) Chapter 4
- (D) Chapter 5

B. If you wanted to read about the cave paintings found at Lascaux, you should begin reading on –

- (A) page 3
- (B) page 31
- (C) page 55
- (D) page 115

Tips and Reminders

- Use key words and phrases in the question to figure out what information is needed.

- Study each part of a book or other visual aid carefully and use it to find the information you need.

PRACTICE

Directions: Choose the best answer to each question about locating information and writing reports.

1. In which reference source should you look to find information on bears found in North America?

- (A) dictionary
- (B) atlas
- (C) encyclopedia
- (D) almanac

2. To find information about Mexican artist Diego Rivera, you should look in the encyclopedia under –

- (A) Mexican
- (B) artist
- (C) Diego
- (D) Rivera

3. Which reference source should you use to find a list of current Senators in the U.S. Congress?

   (A) encyclopedia

   (B) social studies textbook

   (C) biographical dictionary

   (D) almanac

4. Which reference source should you use to find a list of magazine articles about the Olympic Games?

   (A) almanac

   (B) periodicals index

   (C) online card catalog

   (D) encyclopedia

5. Which information needed for a report on Egypt would be found in an atlas?

   (A) the main exports of Egypt

   (B) a history of Egypt

   (C) a map of the Nile River region

   (D) a discussion of Egypt's economy

6. Which reference source should you use to find the origin of the word *gerrymander?*

   (A) science textbook

   (B) thesaurus

   (C) periodicals index

   (D) dictionary

7. If you were assigned to write a social studies report on Africa, which would be the most specific topic?

   (A) Independent African Nations

   (B) History of Africa

   (C) The Economy of Nigeria

   (D) Geography of Africa

8. From the sentences below, which information should be included in research notes for a report on agriculture in China?

   China's population of about one billion people is the largest of any nation in the world. China's farmers produce enough food for this huge population, even though only about 12 percent of the land is suitable for farming.

   (A) population of one billion

   (B) largest of any nation

   (C) produced by Chinese farmers

   (D) 12% of land suitable for farming

9. A list of reference sources used in writing a report would be found in –

   (A) a bibliography

   (B) an index

   (C) a table of contents

   (D) a summary

Directions: Use this outline for a report on movie-making to answer questions 10–13.

Making Movies

I. Movie Jobs
  A. Producer
  B. Director
  C. _____
  D. Editor
  E. Cinematographer

II. Technical Support
  A. Lighting and sound
  B. Set design
  C. Costumes
  D. Special effects
    1. _____
    2. Explosions
    3. Stunts

III. _____
  A. Silent films
  B. Early "talkies"
  C. Color films
  D. Modern movies
    1. Documentaries
    2. Epics
    3. Adventure and drama
    4. _____
    5. Science fiction

10. Line I.C. is blank. Which topic best fits in the blank?

Ⓐ Acting techniques
Ⓑ Home video
Ⓒ Screenwriter
Ⓓ Academy Awards

11. Which topic best fits in the blank beside II.D.1.?

Ⓐ Animation
Ⓑ Costume design
Ⓒ Movie locations
Ⓓ Wide-screen theaters

12. Which sentence would most likely be included in the part of the report based on section II of the outline?

Ⓐ In recent years, many actors have directed their own films.
Ⓑ The first popular cartoons were produced by Walt Disney.
Ⓒ Charlie Chaplin was a star during the silent film era.
Ⓓ The sound track is recorded separately and added to the film.

13. Which heading best fits part III?

Ⓐ Actors and Actresses
Ⓑ Black and White Film
Ⓒ Camera Angles
Ⓓ History of Motion Pictures

Directions: Use this part of an index and bibliography from a social studies textbook to answer questions 14–18.

INDEX

Inchon (*see* **Korea**)
Indochina, 516, 520–523
Indus River Valley,
    civilization of, 360–361
    economy of, 364–365
    geography of, 362–363
    Mohenjo-Daro in, 361–365
Industrial Revolution,
    in Asia, 428–430
    in Europe, 420–424
    in North America, 425–427
International Date Line, 609
Iran, 245–249 (*See also* **Persia**)
Iron Curtain, 490–492

BIBLIOGRAPHY ENTRIES

Anderson, Claude. *Asia's Golden Triangle.*
    Chicago: Asian Press, 1996.
Bolton, Mark. *Imperialism in Africa.* Seattle:
    Historic Press, Inc., 1995.
Chiarro, Ramon. *Meso-American*
    Civilizations. Austin: University Press
    Publishers, 1997.
Chutney, Eunice. *The Slave Trade:*
    1500–1800. Boston: Liberation Press,
    1992.

14. On which pages would you find information about the civilization of the Indus River Valley?

(A) pp. 360–361   (C) pp. 490–492
(B) pp. 364–365   (D) pp. 520–523

15. To find additional information about Iran, you should look under –

(A) Korea   (C) Iron Curtain
(B) Indochina   (D) Persia

16. On which pages should you look for information about the Industrial Revolution in England?

(A) pp. 361–365   (C) pp. 425–427
(B) pp. 420–424   (D) pp. 428–430

17. Which book listed in the bibliography probably has information about the Aztec and Maya in Central America?

(A) *Asia's Golden Triangle*
(B) *Imperialism in Africa*
(C) *Meso-American Civilizations*
(D) *The Slave Trade: 1500–1800*

18. Which author wrote about slavery?

(A) Claude Anderson
(B) Mark Bolton
(C) Ramon Chiarro
(D) Eunice Chutney

PRACTICE 27 • Solving Problems

Directions: Choose the best answer to each problem.

SAMPLES

A. There are 24 jars of jelly in a case and 4 jars in a box. Which number sentence can be used to find how many boxes are in a case?

- Ⓐ $24 \times 4 = \square$
- Ⓑ $24 \div 4 = \square$
- Ⓒ $4 \div \square = 24$
- Ⓓ $24 \times \square = 4$

B. Rita scored 3 times as many goals as Nell during the soccer season. What do you need to know to find how many goals Rita scored?

- Ⓐ how many goals were scored by the whole team
- Ⓑ who scored the most goals
- Ⓒ how many goals Nell scored
- Ⓓ the number of games the team won

Tips and Reminders

- Underline or jot down important information to help you answer each question.

- Check each answer choice before choosing an answer.

- Draw a picture if it helps you answer the question.

- When a question asks <u>about</u> how many or how much, use rounding or compatible numbers to estimate the answer.

PRACTICE

1. Juan reads about 33 pages of a novel in an hour. If he reads for $3\frac{2}{3}$ hours, <u>about</u> how many pages will he read?

- Ⓐ 80
- Ⓒ 120
- Ⓑ 100
- Ⓓ 140

2. Kim bought a sweater on sale at 30% off the regular price. If the sweater originally cost $19.99, <u>about</u> how much did Kim save?

- Ⓐ $3.00
- Ⓒ $5.00
- Ⓑ $4.00
- Ⓓ $6.00

3. Eliza began piano practice at 4:00 P.M. It took her 15 minutes to walk home after practice. What do you need to know to find what time she got home?

Ⓐ what time she left for practice

Ⓑ how long she practiced

Ⓒ how many pieces she played

Ⓓ how fast she walks

4. An auditorium has 34 rows of seats with 52 seats in each row. Which number sentence can be used to find how many seats it has in all?

Ⓐ $34 \times 52 = \square$

Ⓑ $52 \div 34 = \square$

Ⓒ $52 - 34 = \square$

Ⓓ $34 + 52 = \square$

5. Mark made 2 quarts of juice in a glass pitcher. Then he drank 4 glasses. What other information do you need to find how much juice was left?

Ⓐ how much juice a glass holds

Ⓑ how much the pitcher weighs

Ⓒ how much the pitcher holds

Ⓓ what kind of juice he made

6. Jim's house is $2\frac{7}{8}$ miles from school. Selena's house is half as far from school. <u>About</u> how far from school is Selena's house?

Ⓐ 1 mile   Ⓒ 2 miles

Ⓑ $1\frac{1}{2}$ miles   Ⓓ $2\frac{1}{4}$ miles

7. A rectangular room measures 12.5 feet by 9 feet. Which number sentence could you use to find the perimeter of the room?

Ⓐ $(12.5 \times 2) + (9 \times 2) = \square$

Ⓑ $(12.5 - 9) \times 2 = \square$

Ⓒ $(12.5 + 9) \div 2 = \square$

Ⓓ $(12.5 + 2) \times (9 + 2) = \square$

8. Mrs. Garcia bought 15 yards of ribbon. When she finished making award ribbons, she had $6\frac{1}{2}$ yards left. Which number sentence could be used to find how many yards of ribbon she used?

Ⓐ $\square - 15 = 6\frac{1}{2}$

Ⓑ $15 + 6\frac{1}{2} = \square$

Ⓒ $\square \div 6\frac{1}{2} = 15$

Ⓓ $15 - \square = 6\frac{1}{2}$

9. Walt earns $15.00 per hour mowing lawns. Last Saturday, Walt made $52.50 mowing lawns. What question can you answer with this information?

Ⓐ How long does it take Walt to mow one lawn?

Ⓑ How many lawns did Walt mow last Saturday?

Ⓒ How many hours did Walt work last Saturday?

Ⓓ At what time did Walt finish mowing lawns last Saturday?

10. Pens cost $0.79 each or 3 for $2.00. Which number sentence could be used to find the cost of 7 pens?

   Ⓐ $7(\$0.79 + \$2.00) = \square$
   Ⓑ $2(\$2.00) + \$0.79 = \square$
   Ⓒ $3(\$2.00) + 4(\$0.79) = \square$
   Ⓓ $7 \times \$0.79 = \square$

11. Mrs. Hertz needs 300 plastic forks for a party. There are 15 forks in a package. Which number sentence could be used to find how many packages of forks she needs?

   Ⓐ $300 \div 15 = \square$
   Ⓑ $\square \div 15 = 300$
   Ⓒ $300 \times \square = 15$
   Ⓓ $300 - 15 = \square$

12. A bridge has a load limit of 20 tons. A truck weighing 8 tons and carrying cargo is approaching the bridge. What else do you need to know to determine whether the truck will exceed the load limit?

   Ⓐ how tall the bridge is
   Ⓑ how much the truck can carry
   Ⓒ how much the cargo weighs
   Ⓓ how tall the truck is

13. Ernesto wants to make 25 quarter-pound hamburgers for a cookout. Which number sentence should he use to find how much hamburger to buy?

   Ⓐ $25 \times 4 = \square$
   Ⓑ $\square \times \frac{1}{4} = 25$
   Ⓒ $25 \times \frac{1}{4} = \square$
   Ⓓ $25 \div \square = 4$

14. On Tuesday, a stake showed 8.2 in. of snow on the ground. On Wednesday, the measurement was 2.6 in. lower. On Thursday, 4.8 in. of new snow fell. Which number sentence could be used to find how much snow was then on the ground at the stake?

   Ⓐ $(8.2 + 2.6) + 4.8 = \square$
   Ⓑ $(8.2 + 4.8) + 2.6 = \square$
   Ⓒ $(8.2 - 4.8) + 2.6 = \square$
   Ⓓ $(8.2 - 2.6) + 4.8 = \square$

15. On Saturday, the Cree-mee Stand sold 820 ice cream cones. About 70% of them were vanilla and the rest chocolate. Each cone holds 6 ounces of ice cream. Which number sentence could you use to find how many ounces of chocolate ice cream were sold that day?

   Ⓐ $(820 \times 0.3) \div 6 = \square$
   Ⓑ $(820 \times 0.3) \times 6 = \square$
   Ⓒ $(820 \times 0.7) \div 6 = \square$
   Ⓓ $(820 \times 0.7) \times 6 = \square$

16. One issue of a 96-page magazine contains $32\frac{1}{2}$ pages of advertising. Advertisers pay $350.00 for a $\frac{1}{4}$-page ad, $800.00 for a $\frac{1}{2}$-page, and $2000.00 for a full page. What else do you need to know to determine how much money the magazine earned from advertisers?

   Ⓐ why a $\frac{1}{2}$-page ad costs more than two $\frac{1}{4}$-page ads
   Ⓑ what the magazine is about
   Ⓒ the name of the magazine
   Ⓓ how many of each size ad were sold

PRACTICE 28 • Making Judgments

SAMPLES

Directions: Read this letter to the editor. Then answer the questions.

To the Editor:

If you happen to watch the Olympic Games on television in the United States, you might think that the only athletes competing in the Games are Americans. I am French, but I live in Washington, D.C. During the 1994 Olympics in Lillehammer, Norway, and the 1998 Olympics in Nagano, Japan, American TV covered only those events in which Americans stood a good chance of winning. When the American athletes fell behind, the coverage ended. In other countries, TV stations choose which events to cover and then cover the whole event, regardless of whether American athletes are in contention. American TV should provide more balanced coverage of the Olympics. After all, these games are for the whole world.

A. What problem does the writer describe?

Ⓐ The United States needs better athletes for the Olympics.

Ⓑ American TV coverage of the Olympic Games is unfair.

Ⓒ Americans should not be allowed to win so many Olympic medals.

Ⓓ Too few Americans understand other countries.

B. The writer's main purpose in this letter is to –

Ⓐ encourage more people to watch the Olympic Games

Ⓑ complain about American TV coverage of the Olympics

Ⓒ suggest new Olympic sports

Ⓓ entertain readers

Tips and Reminders

• To decide on the author's purpose or point of view, think about what the author is trying to say, how the author feels about the subject, or why the author wrote the passage.

• To make a judgment or decision, think about the information in the passage. Look at all the answer choices and choose the most likely or most important one.

PRACTICE

Directions: Read this passage about Chesapeake Bay. Then answer questions 1–6 on the next page.

In 1997, scores of Chesapeake Bay fishermen fell ill and thousands of dead fish floated into and across the bay. Scientists who studied the outbreak concluded that the cause was a type of algae called *Pfiesteria piscicida*. This algae thrives on the nutrients flowing into the bay from human sources, such as lawn fertilizer and wastewater treatment plants. Many consumers panicked when they heard this news and stopped buying shellfish from the Chesapeake.

Over the past ten years, our nation's largest estuary has developed some serious problems, mainly as a result of overfishing and environmental pollution. Virginia and Maryland have worked hard to curb the amount of pollution flowing into the bay. But their efforts have not been enough. Pollution and silt have clogged the bay, dirtied the water, and destroyed local species, such as rockfish.

Many scientists now believe that the best way to solve the problems in the Chesapeake is to support the growth of its most famous product: oysters. The Chesapeake once supported huge populations of oysters and other bivalves. In fact, the name Chesapeake means "great shellfish bay" in the Algonquian language. Oysters act as wonderfully efficient water filters. At one time, there were so many oysters in the Chesapeake that they could purify all the water in the bay in a matter of days. Now, the oyster population is so low that it would take over a year to achieve the same feat.

Virginia and Maryland are both working to re-establish oyster beds in the Chesapeake, but experts say that more must be done. One scientist suggests banning the harvesting of oysters from one quarter of the oyster beds to protect them from overfishing. That approach is unlikely to succeed, however, because the bay's politically powerful oystermen will not agree to it. They blame natural cycles and diseases, not overharvesting, for the problems in the bay. Perhaps we could help both the oystermen and the bay by paying the oystermen not to fish until the bay at least begins to recover.

Go On

1. According to the author of this passage, what is the main problem in the Chesapeake Bay?

   Ⓐ The area is overcrowded.

   Ⓑ The rockfish have disappeared.

   Ⓒ Too many boats use the bay.

   Ⓓ The bay is polluted.

2. Which is the most serious event that has occurred in the Chesapeake?

   Ⓐ A type of algae has caused illness among fishermen and killed thousands of fish.

   Ⓑ There are not as many oysters as there used to be.

   Ⓒ Virginia and Maryland have not re-established oyster beds.

   Ⓓ The oystermen refused to support the idea of setting aside and protecting oyster beds.

3. The author's main purpose in this passage is to –

   Ⓐ criticize Virginia and Maryland

   Ⓑ encourage people to buy and eat more shellfish

   Ⓒ provide information about Chesapeake Bay

   Ⓓ persuade oystermen to stop fishing

4. According to many scientists, the best solution to the problems in the Chesapeake is to –

   Ⓐ ban all fishing in the bay

   Ⓑ increase the population of oysters

   Ⓒ prohibit boats from using the bay

   Ⓓ ban the use of fertilizers

5. The author of this passage would most likely agree with which of the following statements?

   Ⓐ The Chesapeake is the still the cleanest, most productive body of water in the nation.

   Ⓑ All oyster beds in the bay should be closed to fishing.

   Ⓒ Virginia and Maryland are working to save the bay, but their efforts are not enough.

   Ⓓ Eventually, the human population will die out as a result of its own pollution.

6. According to this passage, which people are most at fault for the decline of the oyster population in the Chesapeake?

   Ⓐ scientists

   Ⓑ recreational boaters

   Ⓒ factory owners

   Ⓓ oyster fishermen

Directions: Read this editorial about children's books. Then answer questions 7–10.

No one in the history of our nation has done more for children learning to read than Theodore Geisel, better known as Dr. Seuss. Who among us has not been entertained by the Cat in the Hat, Bartholomew, and the Grinch–all Dr. Seuss characters.

Before writing his famous children's books, Theodore Geisel worked on movies in Hollywood, and two of his works had won Academy Awards. But it was the publication of *The Cat in the Hat* in 1957 that made Dr. Seuss a household name. That book sold over a million copies in its first three years.

But now, things have changed. Let's compare today's children's books with those of Dr. Seuss. Very few of them have any nonsense words or silly rhymes, or even any sense of fun. Children's books today are too serious! Children need to enjoy reading and enjoy learning new words. English is a marvelous language, but not to children who have to read the same one-syllable boring words over and over again in their books.

In memory of the incomparable Dr. Seuss, let's bring fun back to children's books. Put today's author-Grinches back on the shelf where they belong and bring laughter back to literature.

7. Which statement best reflects the writer's point of view?

   Ⓐ Theodore Geisel should have stayed in Hollywood.

   Ⓑ Dr. Seuss was a wonderful writer and illustrator.

   Ⓒ *The Cat in the Hat* is a ridiculous book.

   Ⓓ No one could ever really believe in the Grinch.

8. According to the writer, what is the problem with children's books of today?

   Ⓐ They are too long.

   Ⓑ They contain nonsense words.

   Ⓒ They use silly rhymes.

   Ⓓ They are too serious.

9. The writer suggests that the problems in today's children's literature can be solved by writing books that –

   Ⓐ use bigger words

   Ⓑ make children laugh

   Ⓒ are more realistic

   Ⓓ have more pictures

10. The author's main purpose in this passage is to –

   Ⓐ persuade

   Ⓑ inform

   Ⓒ explain

   Ⓓ describe

Language Arts

PRACTICE 29 • Reference Materials

SAMPLES

Directions: Use the chart to answer questions A and B.

Winners of the Indianapolis 500

Year	Driver	Car	Time	Speed (mph)
1915	Ralph DePalma	Mercedes	5:33:55.51	89.84
1935	Kelly Petillo	Gilmore Special	4:42:22.71	106.240
1955	Bob Sweikert	John Zink Special	3:53:59.13	128.209
1975	Bobby Unser	Jorgenson Eagle-Offenhauser	2:54:55.08 (435 miles)	149.213
1995	Jacques Villeneuve	Reynard-Ford	3:15:17.561	156.616

A. Who won the Indianapolis 500 in 1955?

  Ⓐ John Zink

  Ⓑ Kelly Petillo

  Ⓒ Bob Sweikert

  Ⓓ Bobby Unser

B. From this chart, what can you conclude about the Indianapolis 500 from 1915 to 1995?

  Ⓐ It has become more popular.

  Ⓑ Speeds have increased.

  Ⓒ The race lasts longer.

  Ⓓ Fewer drivers compete.

Tips and Reminders

- Look for key words to help answer each question.
- Study the reference material carefully and use it to find the information you need.

PRACTICE

Directions: Use this part of a dictionary page to answer questions 1–5.

---

order • orphan

or•gan (ôr'gən) *n.*, **1.** A musical instrument that has several sets of pipes. **2.** Any part of an animal or plant that is made up of different kinds of tissues organized to perform a particular function. **3.** A means for communicating something. **4.** A part of an organization that performs a specific job.

o•ri•ent (ôr'ē ent) *–n.*, **1.** The east. **2.** The Orient, the East; eastern countries. *–v.*, **1.** To place so that it faces in any indicated direction. *Orient the house east and west.* **2.** To adjust to a new situation.

o•ri•gin (ôr'ə jin) *n.*, **1.** Beginning or starting point. **2.** Parentage or birth.

o•rig•i•nal (ə rij'ə nəl) *–adj.*, **1.** First, earliest. **2.** Not copied or imitated; new, fresh. **3.** Inventive; able to do or think new things. *–n.*, Thing from which another is copied or imitated.

or•nate (ôr'nāt) *adj.*, Heavily decorated.

or•ner•y (or'nər ē) *adj.*, Very mean or bad-tempered.

Pronunciation Guide

a pat	ī pie	ə represents
ā pay	o pot	*a* in *a*go
ä father	ō go	*e* in it*e*m
e pet	ô for	*i* in penc*i*l
ē me	u cut	*o* in at*o*m
i pit	û fur	*u* in circ*u*s

---

1. An *ornery* person is –

  (A) heavily decorated

  (B) bad-tempered

  (C) inventive

  (D) not copied or imitated

2. The *a* in *organ* is pronounced like the *a* in –

  (A) pat   (C) ago

  (B) father   (D) pay

3. Which entry word could be found on this same dictionary page?

  (A) ore   (C) orthodox

  (B) ordeal (D) orchard

4. How many syllables are there in *original?*

  (A) 2   (C) 4

  (B) 3   (D) 5

5. Which definition of *orient* fits the way it is used in this sentence?

I need to *orient* myself before I set off to explore the city.

  (A) n. 1   (C) v. 1

  (B) n. 2   (D) v. 2

Directions: Use this screen from a library online catalog to answer questions 6–9.

Library Online Catalog System

Call number SF440.15
S45

Status: Checked out

Author(s) Seibert, Patricia 1959–
Illustrator(s) Jan Davey Ellis
Title Mush! Across Alaska in the longest sled-dog race
Publisher Brookfield, CT The Millbrook Press, c1992
Description 246 pp., pbk., illus.

Subjects 1. Iditarod Trail Sled-dog Race, Alaska. 2. Sled-dog racing.
3. Sled dogs.
I. Ellis, Jan Davey, ill. II. Title

Press <return> to view next screen
Press <delete> to view previous screen

---

6. What is the title of this book?

Ⓐ Sled-dog Racing

Ⓑ Iditarod Trail

Ⓒ Mush! Across Alaska in the Longest Sled-dog Race

Ⓓ Patricia Seibert

7. Which number could you use to locate this book in the library?

Ⓐ 246 pp.

Ⓑ 1992

Ⓒ 1959–

Ⓓ SF440.15

8. This book was published by –

Ⓐ The Millbrook Press

Ⓑ Jan Davey Ellis

Ⓒ Brookfield, CT

Ⓓ Iditarod trail

9. Why would you be unable to take this book out of the library?

Ⓐ It is out of print.

Ⓑ It cannot be removed from the Reference room.

Ⓒ It has no call number.

Ⓓ It has been checked out by someone else.

Directions: Use this table about our solar system to answer questions 10–12.

Planet	Distance from Sun (miles)	Surface Gravity
Mercury	36 million	0.38
Venus	67 million	0.90
Earth	93 million	1.00
Mars	141 million	0.38
Jupiter	484 million	2.64
Saturn	887 million	1.13
Uranus	1.687 billion	1.07
Neptune	2.796 billion	1.08
Pluto	3.668 billion	0.029

10. Which two planets have the same surface gravity?

(A) Earth and Venus

(B) Mercury and Mars

(C) Jupiter and Pluto

(D) Saturn and Neptune

11. How many miles away from the sun is Saturn?

(A) 141 million

(B) 484 million

(C) 887 million

(D) 1.687 billion

12. Earth's surface gravity is closest to that of –

(A) Venus   (C) Mars

(B) Jupiter   (D) Uranus

Directions: Use this supermarket ad to answer questions 13–14.

DIAMOND FOOD STORES

• Super Shoppers •

ULTRA-BUYS OF THE WEEK!

Soak-Up Paper Towels
3 rolls for $2.00

RainFresh Shampoo/Conditioner
89¢ each

EVERYDAY LOW PRICES

Diamond Brand   **Harvest Fresh**
Canned Soup   Yellow Onions
33¢/can   28¢/pound

Weekly Specials
Chicken Wings $3.98
ColdAde $1.29

DIAMOND PHOTO PROCESSING
$3.50/roll with coupon*
(24-exposure roll)

---

13. Which is an "Ultra-Buy" this week?

(A) ColdAde

(B) Canned Soup

(C) RainFresh Shampoo

(D) Chicken Wings

14. You need a coupon to get the special price on –

(A) Soak-Up Paper Towels

(B) Yellow Onions

(C) Chicken Wings

(D) Diamond Photo Processing

PRACTICE 30 • Word Problems

Directions: Solve each problem.

SAMPLES

A. At Toys 4 U, video games are on sale for 25% off. If the regular price of a game is $59.00, what is the sale price?

   Ⓐ $14.75

   Ⓑ $34.00

   Ⓒ $44.25

   Ⓓ $47.20

B. A machine prints 24 cardboard boxes in 2 minutes. At this rate, how long will it take to print 1800 boxes?

   Ⓐ 6 hr

   Ⓑ 2 hr 30 min

   Ⓒ 1 hr 30 min

   Ⓓ 1 hr 15 min

Tips and Reminders

- Figure out what you have to do in each problem and write a number sentence to help you find the answer.

- Draw a picture or make a table if it will help you solve the problem.

- If you have trouble solving the problem, try each answer choice to see which one works.

PRACTICE

1. Ahmed ran the 50-yard dash 5 times. His times were 6.1, 5.8, 5.4, 5.9, and 5.5 seconds. What was his average time?

   Ⓐ 5.74 sec

   Ⓑ 5.82 sec

   Ⓒ 7.18 sec

   Ⓓ 28.7 sec

2. Jane buys 2 sandwiches at $4.75 each and 2 drinks at $1.25 each. How much change should she receive if she gives the clerk $20.00?

   Ⓐ $11.50

   Ⓑ $10.75

   Ⓒ $9.25

   Ⓓ $8.00

3. Melvin works at Pizza Tower. He earns $5.25 per hour. How many hours will he have to work to earn $85.00?

   Ⓐ 15 hr   Ⓒ 17 hr
   Ⓑ 16 hr   Ⓓ 18 hr

4. Mrs. Ames planted $\frac{1}{4}$ of her garden on Tuesday, $\frac{1}{3}$ on Wednesday, and $\frac{3}{8}$ on Thursday. What fraction of her garden did she plant in 3 days?

   Ⓐ $\frac{2}{3}$ Ⓒ $\frac{15}{16}$
   Ⓑ $\frac{11}{12}$ Ⓓ $\frac{23}{24}$

5. Colette walks about 3.2 miles per hour. At this rate, about how long will it take her to walk 15 miles?

   Ⓐ $3\frac{1}{2}$ hr

   Ⓑ 4 hr

   Ⓒ $4\frac{1}{2}$ hr

   Ⓓ 5 hr

6. Kendall spent $27.00 for a book on sale. The regular price of the book is $36.00. What percent discount did he get?

   Ⓐ 15%

   Ⓑ 25%

   Ⓒ $33\frac{1}{3}$%

   Ⓓ 75%

7. Maggie delivers flowers for $6.00 an hour, and she sometimes receives tips. On Tuesday she worked $4\frac{1}{2}$ hours and earned a total of $32.75. How much did she collect in tips?

   Ⓐ $5.75   Ⓒ $26.75
   Ⓑ $6.75   Ⓓ $27.00

8. Fonda made $4\frac{1}{2}$ cups of salsa. If one serving is $\frac{1}{4}$ cup, how many servings did she make?

   Ⓐ 9   Ⓒ 15
   Ⓑ 12   Ⓓ 18

9. Of the 640 cars in a parking garage, 30% are white. How many of the cars are white?

   Ⓐ 213   Ⓒ 182
   Ⓑ 192   Ⓓ 21

10. Esteban bought 50 fence posts. Each post is 6 ft long. If he buries each post 2 ft deep, how much must he cut off the top of each post to make a fence that is $3\frac{1}{2}$ ft high?

    Ⓐ 6 in.

    Ⓑ 8 in.

    Ⓒ 1 ft

    Ⓓ $1\frac{1}{2}$ ft

Use the price list to answer 11–13.

Product	Price
XL Computer	$1350.00
CZ Computer	$995.50
Monitor	$325.00
Color printer	$489.00
Inkjet printer	$345.00

11. What is the total price for an XL Computer, Monitor, and Color printer, not including tax?

Ⓐ $1809.00

Ⓑ $1839.00

Ⓒ $2020.00

Ⓓ $2164.00

12. How much more is the XL Computer than the CZ Computer?

Ⓐ $344.50   Ⓒ $354.50

Ⓑ $345.50   Ⓓ $355.50

13. If the sales tax is 8%, what is the tax on an Inkjet printer?

Ⓐ $25.20   Ⓒ $28.60

Ⓑ $27.60   Ⓓ $43.13

14. In the first four class periods on Friday, Anwar has art, social studies, gym, and math. He does not have gym in the first period or the last. He does not have art second or third. He goes to art class right after math. What class does he have first?

Ⓐ gym

Ⓑ math

Ⓒ social studies

Ⓓ art

15. In a carnival game, there are 60 plastic ducks floating in a pool. The ducks are numbered 1–60. If you choose one duck at random, what is the probability that the duck's number will be less than 16?

Ⓐ $\frac{1}{4}$ Ⓒ $\frac{1}{15}$

Ⓑ $\frac{1}{5}$ Ⓓ $\frac{16}{60}$

16. Five students recorded their weights: 104 lb, 120 lb, 116 lb, 125 lb, 130 lb. What is their average weight?

Ⓐ 116 lb

Ⓑ 119 lb

Ⓒ 120 lb

Ⓓ 122 lb

17. Lenny bought 7 granola bars. If each bar weighs $2\frac{1}{4}$ ounces, how many ounces of granola bars did he buy in all?

    Ⓐ 15 oz

    Ⓑ $15\frac{1}{4}$ oz

    Ⓒ $15\frac{3}{4}$ oz

    Ⓓ 16 oz

18. A postal machine sorts 100 pieces of mail in 30 seconds. At this rate, how long will it take the machine to sort 3500 pieces of mail?

    Ⓐ $17\frac{1}{2}$ min

    Ⓑ $18\frac{1}{2}$ min

    Ⓒ 24 min

    Ⓓ 35 min

19. Ramon buys souvenir coffee mugs for $2.45 each and sells them for $3.95 each. How much profit will he earn if he sells 80 of these mugs?

    Ⓐ $40.00   Ⓒ $196.00

    Ⓑ $120.00   Ⓓ $316.00

20. When Jolene went to the circus, she spent 75% of her money for admission. If admission costs $9.75, how much money did she start with?

    Ⓐ $13.00   Ⓒ $12.50

    Ⓑ $12.75   Ⓓ $7.31

21. Terrell takes the 7 o'clock bus to work on Monday, Tuesday, and Friday. Mora takes the same bus on Tuesday, Wednesday, and Thursday, and Leona takes the bus on Monday, Wednesday, and Friday. If Mora is the only one of the three on the bus, what day is it?

    Ⓐ Tuesday   Ⓒ Thursday

    Ⓑ Wednesday   Ⓓ Friday

22. Connie is 14 years 10 months old. Nora is 2 months younger than Connie and 3 months older than Lily. How old is Lily?

    Ⓐ 14 yr 3 mo   Ⓒ $14\frac{1}{2}$ yr

    Ⓑ 14 yr 5 mo   Ⓓ 14 yr 8 mo

23. Theo ordered 10 pizzas for 22 people. If each person ate $\frac{3}{8}$ of a pizza, how much pizza is left?

    Ⓐ $2\frac{3}{4}$ Ⓒ $1\frac{3}{4}$

    Ⓑ $2\frac{1}{4}$ Ⓓ $1\frac{3}{8}$

24. In a bin containing 150 gumballs, 20% of the gumballs are red and 30% are green. If you take one gumball from the bin at random, what is the probability of getting a gumball that is not red or green?

    Ⓐ $\frac{1}{5}$ Ⓒ $\frac{1}{3}$

    Ⓑ $\frac{1}{4}$ Ⓓ $\frac{1}{2}$

READING: Vocabulary

Directions: Find the word that means the same, or almost the same, as the underlined word.

1. to <u>crave</u>

  Ⓐ expect   Ⓒ attract

  Ⓑ detest   Ⓓ desire

2. a generous <u>donation</u>

  Ⓐ gift   Ⓒ enterprise

  Ⓑ request   Ⓓ salary

3. very <u>conspicuous</u>

  Ⓐ hidden   Ⓒ noticeable

  Ⓑ reluctant   Ⓓ observant

4. <u>substantial</u> wealth

  Ⓐ temporary   Ⓒ evident

  Ⓑ inherited   Ⓓ considerable

5. will <u>reprimand</u>

  Ⓐ provoke   Ⓒ distrust

  Ⓑ scold   Ⓓ advise

6. slight <u>apprehension</u>

  Ⓐ worry   Ⓒ dizziness

  Ⓑ fatigue   Ⓓ confidence

Directions: Find the word that means the OPPOSITE of the underlined word.

7. <u>adverse</u> effect

  Ⓐ serious   Ⓒ favorable

  Ⓑ negative   Ⓓ lasting

8. great <u>disdain</u>

  Ⓐ admiration   Ⓒ patience

  Ⓑ scorn   Ⓓ value

9. to <u>simplify</u>

  Ⓐ dismiss   Ⓒ rearrange

  Ⓑ complicate   Ⓓ evaluate

Directions: Read the two sentences. Find the word that best fits the meaning of **both** sentences.

10. Everyone can _____ from regular exercise.

The Lion's Club hosted a _____ ball to raise money for the homeless.

  Ⓐ charity   Ⓒ benefit

  Ⓑ recover   Ⓓ tire

11. Kenny likes to draw cartoons in his _____ time.

The lawyer begged the jury to _____ the young man's life.

  Ⓐ free   Ⓒ judge

  Ⓑ spare   Ⓓ examine

12. Please _____ from taking pictures during the performance.

The poem's sad _____ set the mood for the rest of the poem.

- (A) verse
- (B) hesitate
- (C) lament
- (D) refrain

13. The first player rolled the _____ and got a seven.

You must _____ these carrots before adding them to the stew.

- (A) dice
- (B) money
- (C) slice
- (D) card

Directions: Read the sentence and the question. Find the word that best answers the question.

14. The dissatisfied customer _____ a refund.

Which word suggests that the customer spoke with authority?

- (A) requested
- (B) expected
- (C) demanded
- (D) begged

15. The police _____ the thief before he could escape.

Which word suggests that the police used force?

- (A) arrested
- (B) seized
- (C) caught
- (D) approached

Directions: Read the sentences. Choose the word that best completes the meaning of each sentence.

Josie stayed up late studying for an algebra ___(16)___. She practiced writing equations and solving ___(17)___ problems. The next morning, Josie was so tired she could ___(18)___ keep her eyes open during the test. She scored ___(19)___ well, but not as well as she had hoped. Although her grade showed some ___(20)___ over the previous test, Josie was still disappointed. She vowed to study harder and get more rest the next time.

16.
- (A) exam
- (B) inspection
- (C) module
- (D) application

17.
- (A) personal
- (B) mathematical
- (C) grammar
- (D) social

18.
- (A) easily
- (B) carefully
- (C) necessarily
- (D) barely

19.
- (A) reasonably
- (B) accordingly
- (C) exceedingly
- (D) temporarily

20.
- (A) outcome
- (B) adjustment
- (C) improvement
- (D) extension

READING: Comprehension

Directions: Read each passage. Choose the best answer to each question.

Horse of a Different Color

Zebras and horses belong to the same genus, *Equus*. Like all horses, zebras have long, handsome faces. Their ears, however, are larger and their manes are stiffer than those of horses. Although zebras, like horses, have strong bodies and long slender legs, the zebras are shorter and their hooves are smaller. The major difference between horses and zebras, though, is stripes. Only zebras have stripes.

The zebra's stripes serve to distinguish it not only from horses, but from other zebras as well. There are three different types of zebras, each with its own special pattern of black or dark brown stripes. The pattern on the zebras' hindquarters helps distinguish one type from another.

No two zebras are exactly alike. Even within a specific type, individual zebras have their own unique stripe patterns. Just like no two human fingerprints are identical, no two zebra stripe patterns are exactly alike. At first glance, all zebras may look the same, but if you look more closely, you'll soon discover that each one is different.

---

21. This passage is mostly about –

Ⓐ what horses look like

Ⓑ three types of zebras

Ⓒ different colors of horses

Ⓓ characteristics of zebras

22. Which statement is an opinion?

Ⓐ Zebras and horses belong to the same genus, *Equus*.

Ⓑ Like all horses, zebras have long, handsome faces.

Ⓒ Zebras are shorter, and their hooves are smaller.

Ⓓ No two zebras are exactly alike.

23. Zebras differ most from horses in that they have –

Ⓐ manes   Ⓒ fingerprints

Ⓑ small ears   Ⓓ stripes

24. Which conclusion can be drawn from this passage?

Ⓐ All animals of the genus *Equus* have stripes.

Ⓑ At first glance, all zebras are noticeably different.

Ⓒ Stripe patterns can be used to identify individual zebras.

Ⓓ Fingerprints are a unique characteristic of some zebras.

Shady Business

Freddie turned his entire room upside down but couldn't find his sunglasses anywhere. The last time he remembered seeing them was a few nights ago when Dustin had spent the night. The two boys had been pretending they were famous rock stars. Freddie played the drums while Dustin, wearing Freddie's sunglasses, played bass guitar and pretended to be the lead singer. Freddie found himself wondering if Dustin had stolen the sunglasses. He quickly dismissed the thought. Dustin just wasn't the type of person that stole from his friends. Or was he? Freddie simply did not want to believe that his best friend might be a thief.

On his way to school, Freddie wondered how he could tactfully ask Dustin about the sunglasses without letting him know that he suspected him of stealing them. He arrived at the schoolyard just as Dustin was stepping off the bus. Freddie's stomach sank. Dustin was wearing the sunglasses!

When Dustin saw Freddie, he waved and pointed to the glasses. He was grinning from ear to ear. Of all the nerve. Freddie's first reaction was to march right up and snatch the glasses off Dustin's face, but he stopped himself just in time. Dustin was his best friend, after all. If Dustin wanted the sunglasses that badly, why, he could have them, thought Freddie. He only wished that Dustin had asked him first instead of just taking them. He would have gladly given them to him.

Upset, Freddie turned on his heel without acknowledging Dustin's greeting and headed for his locker. While fishing around inside looking for his calculator, Freddie suddenly remembered where he'd left his sunglasses. Sure enough, there they were in his locker underneath a pile of dirty gym clothes and several notebooks.

"What do you think?" asked Dustin, coming up to lean against Freddie's locker. Freddie turned and gave Dustin a weak smile.

"I think . . . I think I'm a complete idiot," said Freddie. "Oh, by the way, I like your new shades." He reached into his locker for his own sunglasses and put them on.

25. What do you think will happen next?

- Ⓐ Freddie will accuse Dustin of stealing his sunglasses.
- Ⓑ The boys will fight over the sunglasses.
- Ⓒ The boys will walk to class wearing their sunglasses.
- Ⓓ Freddie won't be able to find his calculator and will suspect Dustin of taking it.

26. What does this story reveal about Freddie?

- Ⓐ He values material things over friendship.
- Ⓑ He wants to be a famous rock star.
- Ⓒ He sometimes jumps to conclusions and later regrets it.
- Ⓓ He doesn't have many friends.

27. Freddie "turned his entire room upside down" means that he –

- Ⓐ redecorated his room
- Ⓑ searched everywhere
- Ⓒ messed up his room
- Ⓓ turned his furniture and wall hangings upside down

28. This story is narrated by –

- Ⓐ Freddie
- Ⓑ Dustin
- Ⓒ a famous rock star
- Ⓓ an outside observer

29. What upset Freddie most when he believed that Dustin had stolen his sunglasses?

- Ⓐ Dustin could easily afford to buy his own pair.
- Ⓑ Dustin looked better in sunglasses than he did.
- Ⓒ Dustin didn't need to steal them since Freddie would have given them to him if he had only asked.
- Ⓓ Without the sunglasses, he could never become a famous rock star.

30. When did Freddie see Dustin wearing sunglasses that he thought were his?

- Ⓐ after searching in his locker
- Ⓑ when they both arrived at school
- Ⓒ before he got on the school bus
- Ⓓ after he found his calculator

31. What was Freddie's problem in this story?

- Ⓐ Someone had stolen his sunglasses.
- Ⓑ His locker was such a mess that he couldn't find his calculator.
- Ⓒ Dustin would not talk to him.
- Ⓓ He thought his best friend was a thief.

32. The theme of this story is mainly concerned with –

- Ⓐ trust between friends
- Ⓑ being vain
- Ⓒ how to handle anger
- Ⓓ being greedy

A Funny Thing Happened . . .

Humor was lounging under a tree one day when he saw an old man carrying a heavy sack. Humor laughed as the old man trudged past. The old man, bent over from the weight of his burden, glared at him before continuing on his way.

"What's in the sack?" Humor asked, falling into step beside him.

"See for yourself," sighed the old man, laying his burden down. Humor reached into the sack and, one by one, began to pull out the old man's problems. First came Worry, green and moldy from age. Chuckling to himself, Humor tossed Worry over his shoulder. His eyes twinkled as he drop-kicked the old man's Anger into a bush by the side of the road.

Soon the old man was laughing at Humor's jocund antics, his problems all but forgotten. "I can't remember when I've had so much fun," he admitted. When it was time for him to go, the old man thanked Humor as he bent down to pick up his sack. He fell over backwards in surprise, it was so light. Dusting himself off, the old man set off down the road, whistling a happy tune.

No sooner had Humor lay down again to rest than an old woman carrying a heavy sack happened by. "What's in the sack?" asked Humor, chuckling softly to himself for he already knew the answer.

33. The author's main purpose in this passage is to –

   Ⓐ compare youth and old age

   Ⓑ criticize people who worry

   Ⓒ teach a lesson

   Ⓓ describe an old man

34. The old man laughed at "Humor's jocund antics." Jocund means –

   Ⓐ cheerful

   Ⓑ bitter

   Ⓒ vengeful

   Ⓓ selfish

35. The old man walked away whistling because he –

   Ⓐ had played a trick on Humor

   Ⓑ had left his problems behind

   Ⓒ felt embarrassed about falling down

   Ⓓ saw an old woman approaching

36. Which is the best summary of this passage?

   Ⓐ An old man and an old woman carry heavy sacks down the road.

   Ⓑ An old man meets Humor on the road and laughs away all his concerns.

   Ⓒ A young man jokes with an old man and makes him laugh.

   Ⓓ A man named Humor falls down in the road, and a fellow traveler helps him on his way.

LANGUAGE ARTS: Mechanics and Usage

Directions: Read each sentence. Look at the underlined part for a mistake in capitalization, punctuation, or word usage. If you find a mistake, choose the best way to write the underlined part of the sentence. If there is no mistake, fill in the bubble beside answer D, "Correct as is."

1. Joshua <u>is spending</u> all his money before he received his next allowance.

   Ⓐ spending   Ⓒ had spent

   Ⓑ spends   Ⓓ Correct as is

2. Several sparrows <u>flied</u> out of the barn.

   Ⓐ flew   Ⓒ flown

   Ⓑ flying   Ⓓ Correct as is

3. Melissa bought a book of poems and sent <u>them</u> to her best friend.

   Ⓐ it   Ⓒ their

   Ⓑ they   Ⓓ Correct as is

4. Corey likes broccoli <u>lesser</u> of all the vegetables on the menu.

   Ⓐ less   Ⓒ least

   Ⓑ more lesser   Ⓓ Correct as is

5. After skiing all day, Trevor was so tired he <u>could barely</u> stand.

   Ⓐ couldn't barely

   Ⓑ could barely not

   Ⓒ barely couldn't not

   Ⓓ Correct as is

6. <u>Gita who</u> is from Sweden, speaks English fluently.

   Ⓐ Gita–who   Ⓒ Gita: who

   Ⓑ Gita, who   Ⓓ Correct as is

7. We drove to <u>Mt. Vernon,</u> Georgia.

   Ⓐ mt. Vernon,   Ⓒ mt. vernon,

   Ⓑ Mt. Vernon   Ⓓ Correct as is

8. <u>Mr Burns</u> car broke down.

   Ⓐ Mr Burns'   Ⓒ Mr. Burns's

   Ⓑ Mr. Burns   Ⓓ Correct as is

9. She owns <u>Concord travel agency</u>.

   Ⓐ Concord Travel Agency

   Ⓑ Concord Travel agency

   Ⓒ Concord travel Agency

   Ⓓ Correct as is

10. Rick asked, <u>where are my mittens.</u>

    Ⓐ where are my mittens?"

    Ⓑ "Where are my mittens?"

    Ⓒ Where are my mittens.

    Ⓓ Correct as is

11. I just read <u>*to kill a Mockingbird*</u>.

    Ⓐ *to kill a mockingbird*

    Ⓑ *To Kill A Mockingbird*

    Ⓒ *To Kill a Mockingbird*

    Ⓓ Correct as is

Directions: Read the sentences. Find the underlined word that has a mistake in spelling. If there are no mistakes in spelling, fill in the bubble beside answer D, "No mistake."

12. Ⓐ Team <u>morale</u> is low.
    Ⓑ We must <u>motivate</u> the players.
    Ⓒ He expects full <u>partisipation</u>.
    Ⓓ No mistake

13. Ⓐ She put <u>alchohol</u> on the wound.
    Ⓑ It was just a small <u>puncture</u>.
    Ⓒ She wrapped my finger in <u>gauze</u>.
    Ⓓ No mistake

14. Ⓐ The minister preached the <u>sermon</u>.
    Ⓑ Someone else read a <u>psalm</u>.
    Ⓒ Later, the choir sang a <u>hymn</u>.
    Ⓓ No mistake

15. Ⓐ Trina is a <u>vegatarian</u>.
    Ⓑ She eats <u>wholesome</u> food.
    Ⓒ Good <u>nutrition</u> is important.
    Ⓓ No mistake

16. Ⓐ John was the youngest <u>applicant</u>.
    Ⓑ He was nervous in the <u>interveiw</u>.
    Ⓒ Someone else got the <u>promotion</u>.
    Ⓓ No mistake

17. Ⓐ Several parents signed a <u>petition</u>.
    Ⓑ The <u>tuition</u> is too high.
    Ⓒ The <u>wealthyest</u> students go there.
    Ⓓ No mistake

Directions: Find the answer that is a complete sentence written correctly.

18. Ⓐ Seals found in waters near the North Pole.
    Ⓑ Seem to fly underwater.
    Ⓒ Swimming under the ice.
    Ⓓ The seals are looking for food.

19. Ⓐ Probably invented by Syrians.
    Ⓑ Each letter represents a sound, letters combined make words.
    Ⓒ There are twenty-six letters in the English alphabet.
    Ⓓ Easier than Chinese characters.

20. Ⓐ Atlantis was a beautiful island.
    Ⓑ Considered by Plato to be the most beautiful on earth.
    Ⓒ The people of Atlantis became greedy they became dishonest.
    Ⓓ An island swallowed up by the sea.

21. Ⓐ Lightning is a form of electricity it builds up in thunderstorms.
    Ⓑ Scientists still don't know how the electricity builds up.
    Ⓒ Flashing bolts of lightning.
    Ⓓ Can't predict where it will strike.

22. Ⓐ Huge piles of dirty laundry.
    Ⓑ Can't find anything clean to wear.
    Ⓒ Dad washes the clothes Mom throws them in the dryer.
    Ⓓ We all fold our own clothes.

LANGUAGE ARTS: Composition

Directions: Read each paragraph. Then answer the questions that follow.

Paragraph 1

Yet they knew a great deal about the movements of the sun, moon, stars, and planets. They could predict a full moon and when an eclipse would occur. How did these ancient peoples know so much? For one thing, they observed the sky every day. Some ancient civilizations built temples. They also kept records. They kept these records from year to year. Ancient people not only recorded celestial events but were also able to predict celestial events as well.

---

23. What is the best topic sentence for this paragraph?

Ⓐ Astronomers study the movements of objects in the sky.

Ⓑ Modern scientists use telescopes.

Ⓒ Ancient peoples did not have the use of telescopes to study the sky.

Ⓓ Ancient Greeks could predict when an eclipse would happen.

24. What is the best way to combine the sixth and seventh sentences?

Ⓐ They also kept records from year to year.

Ⓑ From year to year they also kept records.

Ⓒ From year to year these records were kept.

Ⓓ They also kept records which were kept from year to year.

25. Which sentence does **not** belong in this paragraph?

Ⓐ How did these ancient peoples know so much?

Ⓑ For one thing, they observed the sky every day.

Ⓒ Some ancient civilizations built temples.

Ⓓ They also kept records.

26. Which is the best way to revise the last sentence?

Ⓐ Ancient people recorded and predicted celestial events well.

Ⓑ Ancient people recorded not only celestial events but predictions, too.

Ⓒ Not only were ancient people able to predict celestial events but even recorded them as well.

Ⓓ Ancient people not only recorded celestial events but were also able to predict them.

Paragraph 2

The secret to staying warm is to wear several layers of loose clothing. The loose clothing helps trap body heat. You can add and remove layers as needed in order to stay warm but not hot. Remember to add layers of clothing *before* you get chilled. Also, since nearly half of your body heat escapes from the top of your head, wear a hat whenever you get cool. It's also important to "fuel" your body to keep it warm. So, drink before you get thirsty and eat before you get hungry.

27. What is the best topic sentence for this paragraph?

(A) Winter camping can be dangerous in extremely cold weather.

(B) Here are some tips to help you ski better this winter.

(C) Are you one of those campers that is afraid of cold weather?

(D) Cold-weather activities can be fun if you know how to stay warm.

28. What is the best way to combine the first and second sentences?

(A) The secret to staying warm is to wear several layers of loose clothing, and the loose clothing helps trap body heat.

(B) The secret to staying warm is to wear several layers of loose clothing to help trap body heat.

(C) The secret to staying warm is to wear several layers of loose clothing especially if the loose clothing helps trap body heat.

(D) The secret to staying warm is to wear several layers of loose clothing, but the loose clothing helps trap body heat.

29. Which sentence would fit best at the end of this paragraph?

(A) As you can see, staying warm is easy if you know how.

(B) Your muscles shiver to help keep you warm.

(C) Many people simply do not know how to stay warm.

(D) As your body cools, it will do what it must to get its temperature back up.

30. The writer's purpose in this paragraph is to —

(A) tell an entertaining story

(B) persuade people to enjoy winter

(C) give information

(D) compare hot and cold weather

LANGUAGE ARTS: Study Skills

Directions: Choose the best answer to each question about finding information.

31. If you wanted to learn about the people of Brazil and their customs, you should look in —

- (A) an almanac
- (B) a dictionary
- (C) an atlas
- (D) an encyclopedia

32. Which of these is a main heading that includes the other topics?

- (A) Archery
- (B) Rowing
- (C) Sport
- (D) Tennis

33. To find a list of books or articles that the author used in writing a particular book, you should look in the —

- (A) title page
- (B) index
- (C) table of contents
- (D) bibliography

34. To find a book about Vasili Kandinsky, a Russian painter, you should look in an online library catalog under —

- (A) Vasili
- (B) Kandinsky
- (C) Russia
- (D) painter

35. The word *melody* might be found on a dictionary page with which guide words?

- (A) mellow/menhaden
- (B) meal/media
- (C) menial/mentor
- (D) megalith/melee

Use the chart to answer questions 36–38.

Academy Award Winners: 1992–1996

Year	Best Picture	Best Director
1992	*Unforgiven*	Clint Eastwood
1993	*Schindler's List*	Steven Spielberg
1994	*Forrest Gump*	Robert Zemeckis
1995	*Braveheart*	Mel Gibson
1996	*The English Patient*	Anthony Minghella

36. What movie won the Academy Award for Best Picture in 1994?

- (A) *Unforgiven*
- (B) *Schindler's List*
- (C) *Forrest Gump*
- (D) *Braveheart*

37. In what year was Anthony Minghella named Best Director?

- (A) 1993
- (B) 1994
- (C) 1995
- (D) 1996

38. Who was named Best Director for the movie *Unforgiven?*

- (A) Clint Eastwood
- (B) Steven Spielberg
- (C) Robert Zemeckis
- (D) Mel Gibson

MATHEMATICS: Concepts and Applications

Directions: Choose the best answer to each question.

1. What is 93,572 rounded to the nearest thousand?

   Ⓐ 90,000   Ⓒ 93,600

   Ⓑ 94,000   Ⓓ 93,570

2. What number is expressed by 5,000,000 + 20,000 + 4000 + 60 + 3?

   Ⓐ 5,246,300   Ⓒ 5,024,063

   Ⓑ 5,204,630   Ⓓ 524,603

3. $(6 \times 10^3) + (2 \times 10^2) + (5 \times 10^1) + (3 \times 10^0) =$

   Ⓐ 6,200,053   Ⓒ 6253

   Ⓑ 62,503   Ⓓ 625.3

4. What number completes this pattern?

4, 10, 22, __?__, 94, . . .

   Ⓐ 35   Ⓒ 57

   Ⓑ 46   Ⓓ 68

5. Which expresses the number 168 in prime factors?

   Ⓐ $2 \times 2 \times 2 \times 3 \times 7$

   Ⓑ $2 \times 3 \times 4 \times 7$

   Ⓒ $3 \times 7 \times 8$

   Ⓓ 12×14

6. What is the least common multiple of 3, 5, and 7?

   Ⓐ 15   Ⓒ 35

   Ⓑ 21   Ⓓ 105

7. What is the square root of 3969?

   Ⓐ 7   Ⓒ 49

   Ⓑ 21   Ⓓ 63

8. Which fraction is least?

   Ⓐ $\dfrac{3}{7}$

   Ⓑ $\dfrac{4}{9}$

   Ⓒ $\dfrac{6}{16}$

   Ⓓ $\dfrac{5}{10}$

9. Which fraction is another name for $11\dfrac{5}{9}$?

   Ⓐ $\dfrac{104}{9}$

   Ⓑ $\dfrac{11}{45}$

   Ⓒ $\dfrac{55}{9}$

   Ⓓ $\dfrac{99}{5}$

10. Which percent has the same value as $\dfrac{3}{20}$?

   Ⓐ 5%

   Ⓑ 15%

   Ⓒ 20%

   Ⓓ 25%

MATHEMATICS: Concepts and Applications (continued)

11. Which number has the greatest value?

    Ⓐ 0.1843   Ⓒ 0.3846

    Ⓑ 0.094   Ⓓ 0.527

12. The **8** in 24.1387 represents –

    Ⓐ 8 tenths

    Ⓑ 8 hundredths

    Ⓒ 8 thousandths

    Ⓓ 8 ten thousandths

13. What is 35.2761 rounded to the nearest hundredth?

    Ⓐ 35.0   Ⓒ 35.28

    Ⓑ 35.3   Ⓓ 35.276

14. Which number is closest to the point on the number line indicated by the arrow?

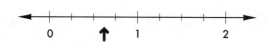

    Ⓐ $\frac{5}{8}$

    Ⓑ $\frac{3}{4}$

    Ⓒ $\frac{1}{2}$

    Ⓓ $\frac{5}{6}$

15. If $6x + 5 = 53$, then $x =$

    Ⓐ 6

    Ⓑ 7

    Ⓒ 8

    Ⓓ 9

16. If $81 \div b = c$, then which of these statements is true?

    Ⓐ $b \times c = 81$

    Ⓑ $c - b = 81$

    Ⓒ $c \times 81 = b$

    Ⓓ $b \div 81 = c$

17. Which number goes in the box to make this sentence true?

$$9(17 + \Box) = (9 \times 17) + (9 \times 5)$$

    Ⓐ 3   Ⓒ 17

    Ⓑ 5   Ⓓ 22

18. Which point on the grid represents $(^-3, 2)$?

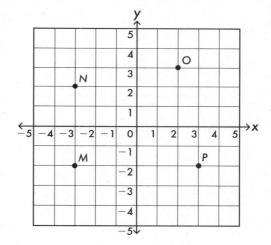

    Ⓐ M   Ⓒ O

    Ⓑ N   Ⓓ P

19. Which two figures are similar?

Ⓐ   Ⓒ

Ⓑ   Ⓓ

20. In this figure, which line segment is parallel to $\overline{DE}$?

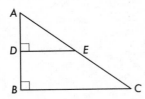

Ⓐ $\overline{AB}$ Ⓒ $\overline{BD}$

Ⓑ $\overline{BC}$ Ⓓ $\overline{AC}$

21. Which type of angle is less than 90°?

Ⓐ acute   Ⓒ right

Ⓑ obtuse   Ⓓ straight

22. What is the perimeter of this parallelogram?

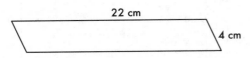

Ⓐ 88 cm   Ⓒ 44 cm

Ⓑ 52 cm   Ⓓ 26 cm

23. What is the area of this triangle?

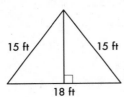

Ⓐ 42 ft²   Ⓒ 108 ft²

Ⓑ 54 ft²   Ⓓ 132 ft²

24. What is the volume of this figure?

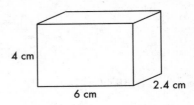

Ⓐ 57.6 cm³   Ⓒ 15.6 cm³

Ⓑ 26.4 cm³   Ⓓ 12.4 cm³

25. If $\angle ABD = 35°$, what is the size of $\angle DBE$?

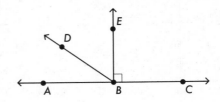

Ⓐ 35°   Ⓒ 45°

Ⓑ 40°   Ⓓ 55°

26. How many inches are there in $3\frac{1}{3}$ yards?

Ⓐ 120 in.   Ⓒ 10 in.

Ⓑ 48 in.   Ⓓ 4 in.

27. Marcy's town went 432 hours without rain. How long is this in weeks and days?

Ⓐ 1 week 4 days

Ⓑ 1 week 5 days

Ⓒ 2 weeks 4 days

Ⓓ 2 weeks 5 days

Directions: Solve each problem. If the correct answer is Not Given, mark answer D, "NG."

28. Jenny's scores on French tests were 89, 75, 94, 99, and 78. What was Jenny's median score?

Ⓐ 87   Ⓒ 96

Ⓑ 89   Ⓓ NG

29. Mrs. Cole ran 5.2 miles in 40 minutes. At this rate, how long would it take her to run 13 miles?

Ⓐ 120 min   Ⓒ 150 min

Ⓑ 135 min   Ⓓ NG

30. Mr. Daniels spends $32.50 on gas every week. If his car gets about 20 miles per gallon of gas, and gas costs between $1.25 and $1.35 per gallon, about how many miles does Mr. Daniels drive each week?

Ⓐ 25 miles   Ⓒ 500 miles

Ⓑ 250 miles   Ⓓ NG

31. The Booster Cub is selling tickets for a drawing. Holly buys 18 tickets and Kevin buys 24. If a total of 378 tickets are sold and 1 ticket is drawn, what is the probability that either Holly or Kevin will win the drawing?

Ⓐ $\frac{1}{50}$ Ⓒ $\frac{1}{9}$

Ⓑ $\frac{1}{42}$ Ⓓ NG

32. At Arthur's, blue jeans that normally cost $31.90 are on sale for 30% off. Kay buys 2 pairs at the sale price. The clerk rings up the total and adds 5% sales tax. How much does Kay pay for each pair of jeans, including tax?

Ⓐ $20.73   Ⓒ $46.89

Ⓑ $23.45   Ⓓ NG

Use the line graph below to answer 33–34.

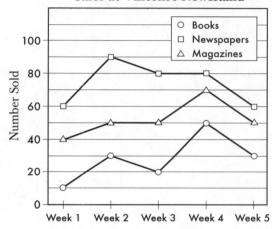

Sales at Vincent's Newsstand

33. In which week were the most magazines sold?

Ⓐ Week 1   Ⓒ Week 3

Ⓑ Week 2   Ⓓ Week 4

34. What was the total number of items sold during Week 3?

Ⓐ 120   Ⓒ 200

Ⓑ 170   Ⓓ NG

MATHEMATICS: Computation

Directions: Find the answer to each problem. If the correct answer is Not Given, mark answer D, "N."

35.
$$52,147 - 48,189$$
- Ⓐ 4968
- Ⓑ 4048
- Ⓒ 3958
- Ⓓ N

36. $129.062 + 21.7341 =$
- Ⓐ 150.7961
- Ⓑ 346.403
- Ⓒ 2302.472
- Ⓓ N

37. $39\overline{)97,347}$
- Ⓐ 2496 R3
- Ⓑ 2496
- Ⓒ 249 R7
- Ⓓ N

38. $22.07 \times 35 =$
- Ⓐ 77,035
- Ⓑ 7704
- Ⓒ 7703.5
- Ⓓ N

39. $\$16.99 \times 14 =$
- Ⓐ $2.38
- Ⓑ $23.79
- Ⓒ $237.86
- Ⓓ N

40. $18.02 \times {}^{-}5 =$
- Ⓐ ⁻901
- Ⓑ 90.1
- Ⓒ 9.01
- Ⓓ N

41. $\frac{19}{6} + 4\frac{3}{4} =$
- Ⓐ $3\frac{11}{12}$
- Ⓑ $6\frac{5}{12}$
- Ⓒ $7\frac{11}{12}$
- Ⓓ N

42. $(^{-}37 + 8) - 2 =$
- Ⓐ ⁻42
- Ⓑ ⁻36
- Ⓒ ⁻31
- Ⓓ N

43. $5.25\overline{)\$573.30}$
- Ⓐ $1092.00
- Ⓑ $109.20
- Ⓒ $10.92
- Ⓓ N

44. $\frac{5}{8} \div \frac{1}{2} =$
- Ⓐ $\frac{5}{16}$
- Ⓑ $\frac{4}{5}$
- Ⓒ $1\frac{1}{4}$
- Ⓓ N

45. $170 = \square\% \text{ of } 680$
- Ⓐ 20
- Ⓑ 25
- Ⓒ 33.3
- Ⓓ N

46. $50\% \text{ of } 299 =$
- Ⓐ 149.5
- Ⓑ 14.95
- Ⓒ 1.495
- Ⓓ N

Stop

Scoring Chart

Name _____ Class _____

Directions: Use this page to keep a record of your work. Make a check mark (✔) beside each test you finish. Then write your test score.

✔ PRETEST	Score	%
Reading	/36	
Language Arts	/38	
Mathematics	/46	
Total	/120	

✔ POST-TEST	Score	%
Reading	/36	
Language Arts	/38	
Mathematics	/46	
Total	/120	

✔ PRACTICE TEST	Score	%
1. Synonyms/Antonyms	/28	
2. Using Verbs	/14	
3. Whole Number Concepts	/16	
4. Context Clues	/24	
5. Grammar and Usage	/10	
6. Fractions, Decimals, and Percents	/15	
7. Word Analysis	/12	
8. Sentences	/20	
9. Number Operations	/10	
10. Interpreting Text	/8	
11. Punctuation	/10	
12. Geometry	/15	
13. Main Idea/Details	/6	
14. Capitalization	/10	
15. Measurement	/14	

✔ PRACTICE TEST	Score	%
16. Text Structure	/12	
17. Spelling	/15	
18. Computation	/30	
19. Inferences	/10	
20. Combining Sentences	/8	
21. Estimation	/12	
22. Literary Elements	/16	
23. Composition	/10	
24. Interpreting Data	/14	
25. Evaluating Information	/10	
26. Study Skills	/18	
27. Solving Problems	/16	
28. Making Judgments	/10	
29. Reference Materials	/14	
30. Word Problems	/24	